W9-CEX-806

THE STORY OF THE SECRET SERVICE

THE STORY
OF THE
SECRET SERVICE

by FERDINAND KUHN

RANDOM HOUSE · NEW YORK

Contents

Foreword

For almost one hundred years the United States
Secret Service has served the people of this country
honestly and effectively. It has fought crime without seeking glory or glamor, and it has won a respected place among law-enforcement agencies of
the world.

It is a good thing for young Americans to know
what is being done to keep law and order in the

United States. It is good for them to learn that fighting crime has become a real profession, with fine possibilities for interesting careers and good futures. The men who enforce the laws today must eventually give way to younger people, and the younger people must not only inherit that responsibility but also must try to do a better job.

On occasion, in magazines, books, movies or television, the hero who solves mysterious murders, recovers vital plans, foils foreign plots, or even captures cattle rustlers, has been identified as a "Secret Service man." Authors of such stories obviously do not know what a real Secret Service man does.

The Secret Service did not ask that this book be written. The author, Mr. Kuhn, came to us and asked if we would furnish information about our duties and about some of our closed criminal cases, as the basis for the book. We had not met Mr. Kuhn, but knew that he had a reputation as an excellent reporter who literally has made the world his "beat," and who gets his facts straight and presents them accurately. We were assured that the real story of the Secret Service would thus not be distorted.

Mr. Kuhn talked with many people in the Secret

Service and learned at first hand how they work. He has not tried to show that they are supermen. They are simply good investigators who work hard to do a conscientious job. Mr. Kuhn shows the men as they really are, and the cases as they actually happened, and for this we are everlastingly grateful.

U. E. Baughman
Chief, U. S. Secret Service

Author's Note

Most of the stories in this book have come from official reports in the Secret Service files. If a central character has gone to jail, his real name appears in these pages. But if he has been put on probation, or sent to a mental hospital or set free, you will know him only by a disguised name. It would not be fair to identify these people more closely.

Chief Baughman and his men have co-operated

in every possible way to make this an authentic "Story of the Secret Service." Mr. Baughman has opened the files to me and has let me choose those individual cases which, in my opinion, would best illustrate the recent work of the Secret Service.

He has allowed me to attend the Secret Service school, to question many of his agents about their work, and to publish pictures which are not usually made available to outsiders. In addition, Mr. Baughman and his staff have been kind enough to check the manuscript for accuracy. The selection and treatment of the material, and the opinions expressed, are mine alone.

I should like to say "Thank you!" not only to the Chief, but also to Joseph J. Ellis, Jr., in charge of the Protective Research Section; to Robert F. Grube, in charge of the Counterfeit Section; to James J. Rowley, in charge of the White House Detail; to William Bouck, director of the Secret Service school; to Louis B. Nichols, assistant to the Director of the Federal Bureau of Investigation, for technical details of fingerprinting; to former Chief Frank J. Wilson and former Director Alvin W. Hall of the Bureau of Engraving and Printing, who shared their memories and their knowledge with me; and especially to Assistant Chief Harry E. Neal, who gave me many hours of patient and willing help.

F.K.

THE STORY OF THE SECRET SERVICE

1
Men Who Carry
the Star-Shaped Badge

"He's coming! He's coming!"

The crowd has been massing along the street for hours. Now it packs every inch of curb space behind the police lines. Heads lean out of every window in every building. From far down the street, thousands hear the sputter of motorcycle exhausts.

"He's coming!"

The President of the United States has come to town and is on his way from the airport.

A motorcycle escort roars slowly past in a cloud of exhaust fumes. Planes streak across the sky in a salute. A long black car rolls by at slightly more than walking pace. The President can be seen standing, waving and bowing, as yells and whistles split the air.

Four young men in civilian clothes stride alongside the Presidential car, one near each fender. They do not look at the President at all. They peer intently, alertly, at the crowd on the street and sometimes at the faces in the windows above.

Behind them two more men stand on the running board of another black car which follows the President's. These men, too, are watching the crowd, and each of them has one hand near his pocket.

The crowd gets thicker as the President approaches the auditorium where he is to make a speech. A woman throws a bouquet of flowers toward the President's car. One of the alert young men leaps for it and catches it as if it were a forward pass in a football game.

The President's car pulls up to the auditorium entrance. All six men cluster around him in a kind of box formation, as he gets out and shakes hands with the welcoming committee.

These are men of the United States Secret Service. Their job on this day, and always, is to protect the President—to prevent anyone from shooting him, or throwing an explosive at him, or even from tossing something as innocent-looking as a bouquet of flowers.

If you should look at these young men, you would think that they were just average, nice-looking Americans. Their clothes are neat, their manner polite but serious. Not one of them barks an order like an army sergeant; not one has the tough, hard look that used to be the mark of a detective.

But Secret Service men are anything but "average." In their training they have come through tests such as few other Americans must meet. In their work they run risks that few others have to face. Their protective duty at Presidential parades is only a trifling part of their day-to-day responsibility.

They not only have to protect the President every minute, day and night, wherever he may be. They also have to find and catch the criminals who imitate, or counterfeit, money, and those other criminals who steal or put false signatures on government checks.

Every Secret Service man is partly a detective, partly a policeman with the power to arrest, and partly a bodyguard. Because these agents have to do so much of their work without calling attention to themselves, people used to call them "The Silent Service."

They do not like to advertise themselves. They seldom talk to strangers about their methods and almost never about their successes. The whole of their story has seldom been written. But over more than ninety years, their service has become the oldest and one of the proudest of the government's law-enforcing agencies.

Although the work of the Secret Service covers the whole of the United States, including Hawaii, Alaska and Puerto Rico, it has fewer than 300 agents. The Secret Service also directs the work of 154 uniformed men in the White House Police Force and seventy others in the Treasury Guard Force, who protect more than fifty billion dollars of money and government bonds in the Treasury buildings in Washington.

How can the Secret Service do its job with so few

men? One answer is that it has tens of thousands of friendly partners: the state and local police in the United States, and often the police of many foreign countries as well. Although its headquarters are in Washington, most of its men are scattered in fifty-seven branches, or field offices, throughout the nation.

Whenever a Secret Service man has an assignment in one of these fifty-seven cities, or in some other, he often asks the city police to help him. Almost always they give their help willingly. City police forces have come to know the Secret Service. They trust and respect it.

And whenever a local policeman or detective has helped to solve a Secret Service case, he gets a message of thanks from the Chief in Washington, and sometimes an Award of Merit from the Secretary of the Treasury and the Chief.

The Secret Service is one of six law-enforcement agencies in the Treasury Department. The others are:

1. The Coast Guard, which patrols coastal waters against smugglers, helps ships in distress, maintains lighthouses and removes dangers to navigation. In wartime it becomes a part of the Navy.

2.   The Customs Service, with inspectors at seaports and other border points to collect customs fees on goods entering the United States.

3.   The Narcotics Bureau, which works with local police and the United Nations to prevent the making or selling of forbidden drugs.

4.   The Treasury Intelligence Unit, of the Internal Revenue Service, which guards against cheating the government of tax money.

5.   The Alcohol and Tobacco Tax Division, of the Internal Revenue Service, which enforces revenue laws relating to alcohol and tobacco. This Division also enforces the National Firearms Act, which requires registration of certain kinds of firearms.

Because the Secret Service is a part of the Treasury, like these other agencies, its men are sometimes known as "T-men." But don't call a Secret Service agent a "T-man" if you want to be popular with him!

Though he would rather be in the Treasury than in any other part of the government, he likes to be called a Secret Service agent—and nothing else. As a symbol of his service and his pride, he carries a leather folder in a trousers pocket. Inside the folder is a star-shaped badge of silver. The two words

"Secret Service" form a circle inside the star. In the center of the circle are the initials "U.S."

To every good agent, this is more than a badge of identity. It is a badge of honor.

Old-time agents turn pale when they think of the tests a young man has to take nowadays to enter the Secret Service. Former Chief Frank J. Wilson, one of the greatest of the veterans, often tells his friends:

"I couldn't get into it today if I had to pass those tests."

He, like other agents of former years, is glad that the standards are so high today.

A man who wants to join the Secret Service must be between 23 and 30 years old, at least five feet eight and not over six feet two in height. He must be in perfect health because a Secret Service man with a chronic sniffle or bad eyesight or other defects would be of little use in an emergency.

Along with others who want Treasury enforcement jobs, he must pass a stiff written examination. But this is less important than an oral test given by a group of sharp-eyed and sharp-eared examiners. The questioners want to know not only how much information a new man may have, but also whether he is self-controlled and clear in speech, and quick in his thinking.

If a candidate passes these tests, the Secret Service checks every scrap of information it can find about him, all the way back to his birth: his family, his friends, his interests, his record in school and college. When it accepts him, he gets his commission and his badge making him a Secret Service agent.

But his training has only begun.

For a year he serves in a Secret Service field office. He learns how to shadow suspected criminals without being seen. He learns to follow up clues, to read fingerprints and to judge the value of every scrap of evidence.

He practises pistol-shooting until he can hit the bull's-eye on a fast-moving target. He makes himself expert in judo, the Japanese system of self-defense without weapons, and learns about firearms and explosives.

In addition, he has to study American law and government so that he never violates the rights of an American citizen. The Secret Service has never lost a case in court on the ground that it used evidence obtained from tapping telephone wires. It never intercepts mail. It trains its men to regard themselves as public servants, to respect the rights of others, and never to think of themselves as being above the law.

For a month of a new agent's first year, he is assigned to the White House Detail in Washington, where about thirty Secret Service men work constantly to protect the President. The best kind of background for a man in this work is a good record in sports.

"Our men don't need to be husky," says James J. Rowley, the agent in charge of the White House Detail. "They need to be flexible, like good football or basketball players. They have to be able to think ahead to what an assassin might do, and forestall him."

Rowley watches these trainees closely during their thirty days at the White House. If he likes the way they do their jobs, he recommends giving them permanent assignments to the White House Detail. In time, such newcomers may be among the men walking alongside the President's car in a parade.

Even after their first year, their training is not over. Every agent must come to Washington for six weeks in the Treasury Enforcement School and five more weeks in the Secret Service School. To help him fight counterfeiting, he must learn how paper money and coins are made, and why. To help him protect the President, he spends several days at a mental hospital, interviewing doctors and learning how to recognize the mentally twisted men and women who might become assassins.

If a recruit proves that he has all the qualities the Secret Service needs, there is no limit to his advancement within the service. To take one example, the present Chief, U. E. Baughman, climbed all the rungs of the ladder, right to the top. Mr. Baughman (pronounced "Bawman") entered the service at 22 as a stenographer. He rose to direct the field offices in Newark, Washington and New York. Then, in 1948, he became Chief at the age of only 43.

Secret Service duty has become a career of a lifetime, a highly trained and specialized profession. And it is a serious profession, sometimes deadly serious. All those who carry the star-shaped badge have pledged themselves, in the words of their instruction book, "to be prepared to sacrifice their lives, if necessary . . ."

Some of them have obeyed this instruction to the limit, as this book will tell.

2
Beginnings of
the Secret Service

There had been a "secret service," a famous one, in the Union army during the Civil War. It was a military agency not related in any way to the civilian Secret Service of today.

Its first leader was Allan Pinkerton, the best-known American private detective of his time. He owed his army job partly to the fact that he had warned Abraham Lincoln of a plot to murder him.

He had seen a barber named Ferrandini wave a long, glittering knife at a secret meeting of Southern sympathizers in Baltimore. The barber had sworn that he would plunge it into Lincoln's heart.

Lincoln was then in Philadelphia, on his way to take the oath of office as President. Pinkerton hurried there to alert him.

"We know, Mr. Lincoln, beyond the shadow of a doubt, that there exists a plot to assassinate you. The attempt will be made on your way through Baltimore, day after tomorrow."

At first Lincoln would not believe it.

"But why—why do they want to kill me?"

"Rebel agents are all over the place," Pinkerton answered. "Nobody in the North can understand what fanatics they are."

Lincoln listened soberly. Then he asked: "What do you propose to do about it?"

"We propose to take you on to Washington this very night and steal a march on your enemies."

Thanks to the warnings by Pinkerton and others, Lincoln agreed to change his schedule. He slipped through Baltimore secretly, at night, in the last car of a darkened railroad train. He was safe in Washington hours before the assassin was to kill him.

Lincoln was grateful. It was natural to put Pinkerton in charge of the "secret service" when the war began.

Pinkerton's men became the eyes and ears of the Union armies. They scouted ahead of the marching columns.

Their spies in the South fed Confederate secrets back to Washington. Their detectives in Northern cities caught Confederate agents by the dozen. Pinkerton resigned after a year and a half of war, but month by month the secret service grew stronger, more accurate, better organized.

Soon its exploits became legends.

One of its agents, a lion-hearted woman named Pauline Cushman, spied her way far behind the Confederate lines. The Southerners captured her and sentenced her to be hanged. But she escaped and made her way back to the Union lines with enough valuable information to trap an entire regiment.

The cheering soldiers called her "Major," and the army let her wear a major's insignia for the rest of the war.

When Lee surrendered at Appomattox, the old military secret service went out of existence. The time for spy work was past. What the government needed now was a civilian detective force to do the quiet, patient work of fighting a special kind of crime.

Criminals had been counterfeiting the money issued by the United States. That is, they had been imitating money and using it as if it were real. In the last two years of the Civil War, a third of all the paper money in circulation was fake money made by criminals. If this deadly game of copying money could not be stopped, the public would lose all confidence in real currency.

Hugh McCulloch, the Secretary of the Treasury under President Andrew Johnson, was frightened at the prospect. He ordered a new United States Secret Service set up within the Treasury Department. Its jobs were to catch the counterfeiters, to scare other criminals away from copying money, and to build up public trust in the nation's currency.

Except for its name, the new service had no connection with the old, but its men would need some of the same qualities of detective skill and daring.

In its early years the Treasury's Secret Service had a hard time. A government that had known how to direct a tremendous Civil War didn't yet know how to fight a continuing war against criminals.

Politicians often filled the jobs for which trained detectives were needed. Some of them did not even know how to shoot. The early Secret Service, like most police forces of those days, did not always obey the legal and ethical rules of law enforcement today.

But sometimes, even in its first years, the Secret Service had well-trained and devoted chiefs. At such times it cracked down hard on counterfeiters. It put scores of them behind prison bars, and alert Secret Service agents were able to capture hundreds of thousands of dollars of bad money. Counterfeiters were tracked down and fought as public enemies.

One dangerous and slippery enemy in 1876 was the Kenealy gang of counterfeiters in Illinois. Ben Boyd, who actually copied the money for the gang, had been caught and jailed for ten years. The gang had no one else who could make imitation money half so cleverly as Boyd; it was helpless without him.

How to get him out of prison? One night, in a secret meeting, a member of the gang came up with a weird idea.

"Do you know where Lincoln's tomb is?" he asked Kenealy, his gang leader.

"Sure, it's in Oak Ridge Cemetery in Springfield. But what's Lincoln's tomb got to do with us?"

"Everything! Nobody guards that tomb at night. We could get Lincoln's body, take it over to Indiana and bury it in a secret place I know in the sand dunes. Then we could get a message to Boyd in prison."

"But what could Boyd do about it?"

"He could say that he knew where the body was hidden. He could name the place—if the Governor would give him a pardon. Then we'd get our friend back again."

The Secret Service had been trailing the Kenealy gang and got wind of the plot. At first the agents in Illinois could not take it seriously. But knowing Kenealy's record, knowing that he would shoot and kill, they also knew that he would not stop at stealing the body of America's national hero.

A telegraph message dot-dashed to Washington. The Chief of the Secret Service decided to consult Robert T. Lincoln, the President's only surviving son, who was soon to be Secretary of War.

"Mr. Lincoln, there's a real plot in Springfield to take your father's body and hold it for ransom. Our men know who the ringleaders are. They are dangerous counterfeiters; we've been trying to catch them for months.

"If we station men around your father's tomb, we can catch these counterfeiters as grave robbers, and they'll get a one-year sentence. But we'd like to have your consent before we do it."

Robert Lincoln agreed—with one condition.

"I wish you would use Allan Pinkerton to help you," he said. "My father had such a friendly feeling toward him. You remember that he helped to save my father's life."

So the new Secret Service telegraphed to the man who had founded the old secret service in wartime. Pinkerton was then in New Orleans, ill and partly paralyzed. He took the first train for Springfield, and agreed with the Secret Service plan to station guards around the Lincoln tomb.

Night after night nothing happened. Then, on November 7, 1876, a pitch-dark night with no moon, two men crept into the cemetery. It was the night of the Hayes-Tilden Presidential election, one of the closest in American history. The Springfield police were busy guarding polling places, but not too busy to have stationed some men, along with the Secret Service agents, among the gravestones.

The robbers at the tomb could be heard straining and heaving to move the great stone block that covered the casket. With crowbars they managed to move the stone eighteen inches.

It was too dark for the agents to see anything. They could only hear the tapping and crunching of steel against stone. They were like people in a dark room who hear a rat gnawing at the floor boards.

A pistol shot broke the stillness. At just the wrong moment, an over-anxious policeman had pulled his trigger.

Others, thinking the criminals were shooting, fired into the darkness, not knowing where to aim.

The cemetery echoed with gunfire. Pistols flashed like giant fireflies without lighting the target.

In the uproar, the criminals got away. But both were caught the next day and sentenced to a year for grave robbery. Soon afterward the Secret Service arrested Kenealy, the leader of the gang, for counterfeiting.

Such exploits brought fame to the new agency. Since it was the only federal detective force doing general investigative work, other government departments took to borrowing its agents from the Treasury.

In the ten-week Spanish-American War, for example, the War Department asked Secret Service agents to find out how the Spaniards were getting so many American military secrets.

The main Spanish fleet was at sea in that summer of 1898. Nobody on this side of the Atlantic knew just where it was. The people of New York and other coastal cities half feared, half expected, that Spanish warships would appear off their harbors any morning and bombard them.

In this atmosphere of excitement and near-panic, the Secret Service discovered that neutral Canada was the headquarters of the main Spanish spy ring. Helped by efficient Canadian police, the agents tracked the spies to Montreal; and the Canadians promptly hustled them out of the country.

This kind of war work was important, no doubt, but it interfered with the war against counterfeiting which was supposed to be the Secret Service job. The overworked agents soon found themselves on many other assignments far outside their Treasury work. Two pistol shots in Buffalo, New York, were to give them their biggest, most solemn and most responsible task.

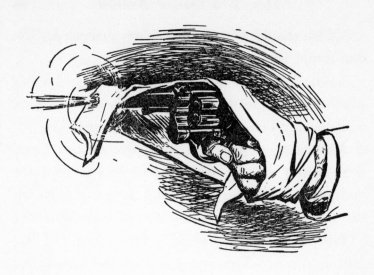

3
Shots
That Shamed America

The President of the United States was on a visit to
a world's fair at Buffalo. He agreed to hold a public
ten-minute reception at which anyone could file past
and shake his hand.

"Please don't do it, Mr. President!" his secretary begged him. "It won't be safe. I wish you
would cancel it."

"Why should I?" the President answered. "No one would wish to hurt me."

So the President took his place in front of a low platform, with potted palms on both sides of him, while a long line of citizens filed past.

Most of them had never laid eyes on this President or any other. They would tell their children and grandchildren about the day they not only saw the President but also shook hands with him.

Fifty uniformed police and soldiers kept the line moving quickly. Two Secret Service men stood near the President, but in those days it was not their business to guard him, and they left this job to the police and soldiers.

A young man in a neat dark suit walked up in the line. His right hand was wrapped in a white handkerchief. The President stretched out his hand.

The young man stretched out his—and fired twice. Hidden in the handkerchief was a revolver.

The President was William McKinley, a man who probably had fewer enemies than any American leader of his day. The date was September 6, 1901. The assassin was Leon Czolgosz (pronounced

"Cholgosh"), a factory worker of Polish parentage.

He was an anarchist who hated all government. He had nothing against McKinley except that the President was head of a government and therefore deserved to be killed.

The President died of his wounds eight days later. Czolgosz was rushed to trial and was shocked to death in the electric chair only forty-five days after the crime. The country, mourning its President, rang with cries that all anarchists be jailed or shipped abroad.

The Secretary of the Treasury promptly ordered the Secret Service to be responsible for protecting the President in the future. This was a historic order in the life of the Secret Service. It was a far graver and harder assignment than chasing counterfeiters. And it was tragically overdue.

When Czolgosz fired through his handkerchief, drilling a fatal wound into McKinley, it was the third time in thirty-six years that a President had been murdered.

Men and women who filed past at Buffalo could remember when John Wilkes Booth had killed Abraham Lincoln in a box at Ford's Theater. Booth, an actor with an insane father, had plotted the crime as revenge for the defeat of the South in the Civil War.

Young people at Buffalo, not long out of college, could remember when Charles J. Guiteau had shot President Garfield in a railroad station in Washington. Guiteau, a mentally-upset lawyer, evangelist and swindler, had been pestering Garfield to appoint him ambassador to Austria or consul in Paris. Garfield, too, had died of his wounds after lingering through weeks of agony.

Even after these tragedies, no President was protected in any but the most casual way. The whole idea of surrounding him with armed guards was somehow foreign and distasteful to the American public. It might be all right for European kings and emperors, but not for the men of the people who were elected to the White House.

Only one magazine, the respected *Independent*, drew the right moral when it commented on the McKinley murder:

"We have learned by the saddest experience— three Presidents murdered in thirty-six years, three times as many as the rulers of Russia or France or Italy—that we must protect our Presidents by the strictest detective care."

Neither the new President, Theodore Roosevelt, nor the leaders of the Secret Service, nor the American public, yet seemed to understand what protection meant. The Secret Service was asked to do a job for which it lacked men, money and experience. When the Secretary of the Treasury first ordered it to protect the President, he added to its staff—two men!

The new President himself didn't believe in being protected by Secret Service agents.

"Of course," he wrote to a friend, "they would not be the least use in preventing an assault upon my life. I do not believe there is any danger of such an assault, and if there were, it would be simple nonsense to try to prevent it.

"For, as Lincoln said, though it would be safer for a President to live in a cage, it would interfere with his business."

Roosevelt wanted the Secret Service, first, to shield him from unwelcome visitors, especially when he was on vacation; and second, to be a detective agency for the government generally.

The federal government had no other general detective force. In Roosevelt's words, an agency like the Secret Service was "by far the most efficient instrument possible to use against crime." It was efficient because it had trained detectives on its staff, it had a permanent place in the government, and it could work separately from local detective forces in the cities.

The great land robberies of 1905 gave T.R. his chance to use the Secret Service as he wished. Decades before, in Civil War days, forty million acres of government-owned land in the West had been thrown open to settlers.

Now Roosevelt had evidence that powerful mining, grazing and lumbering companies had been stealing this land, selling it to others and growing richer on the proceeds. To catch the thieves, Roosevelt asked his Department of Justice to borrow thirty-two Secret Service agents.

What did it matter that these men were supposed to be guarding the President and catching counterfeiters? To Roosevelt, the land frauds were important enough to take Secret Service men off their regular beats for months at a time.

One of these borrowed agents was shot in the back with seventeen shotgun slugs while he was checking the theft of coal from government-owned land. The killers were acquitted—probably because a local judge was too close to the company that had hired them to do the shooting. Other agents plowed ahead getting evidence.

Their trail led them higher, always higher, to important men who were growing rich out of the stealing of public property. A Senator, a Congressman, a Federal District Attorney were among the accused.

Suspicion pointed to so many others in the West that Congress itself grew uneasy. Senators and Representatives began attacking the Secret Service as the President's "spies" snooping into their personal affairs. Finally, Congress defied Roosevelt by passing a law that no government department except the Treasury—not even the Department of Justice—could borrow Secret Service agents.

Roosevelt was furious. He felt Congress had taken the side of the criminals against the public. Without arguing further, he ordered the Department of Justice to set up a brand-new Bureau of Investigation in 1908 to do its own detective work. Secret Service men were transferred to the Department of Justice. This was the birth of what is now the Federal Bureau of Investigation, the F.B.I.

It was also the beginning of better days for the Secret Service. Now, at last, the little agency in the

Treasury was able to do a better job of its own, against counterfeiters and assassins. From that day to this, only one President, Woodrow Wilson, has ordered the Secret Service to do a special job outside its regular duties.

4

The Bulging Brief Case

Frank Burke, of the Secret Service, was an old-fashioned detective.

That is, he didn't always stick to the written rules. He thought books about crime detection were overrated. But as a veteran Secret Service officer, Burke could follow a clue like a bloodhound on a scent.

He never forgot a mole on a face or a scar on a cheek, and he was as quick with his wits as with his gun. The chief of the Secret Service used to turn to Burke whenever he had an especially tricky counterfeiter to catch.

One spring day in 1915, early in the First World War, the Chief sent for him again. It was only a week after a German submarine's torpedo had crashed into the side of the great British liner *Lusitania*, drowning 114 Americans along with more than a thousand other men, women and children.

"Here's something, Frank, that's a little out of our line," the Chief said. "But we'll have to do it."

He lowered his voice to give it a confidential tone:

"President Wilson wants it. He is sure the Germans are plotting explosions in American factories that are making war material for the British and French. But we haven't been able to prove it— yet.

"Of course, we're neutral in this war, but any foreign agent who blows up factories, or pays someone else to do it, is violating our neutrality.

"I think there's a higher-up in this business," the Chief went on. "The President and the Secretary of State think so too. They think he's more important than the German Ambassador. I want you to find out who he is and get all you can on him."

Burke's eyes twinkled. This was the kind of hard and unusual detective job he liked.

"All right, Chief, I'll do my best," he promised.

One of his first moves was to consult a lawyer who knew a good deal about German shipments to this country and the men who ordered them.

"You're right," the lawyer told Burke. "There really is a higher-up in the German organization. He's in New York. I've never seen him, but I know that his name is Dr. Heinrich Albert."

"Have you got a picture of him?" Burke asked.

"No, but I've been told what he looks like. He's six feet one inch tall, fifty years old, about 190 pounds. He has a long nose, a clipped mustache, and two big saber scars on his cheeks—you know, the kind German students give each other in dueling contests."

That was enough for Frank Burke. He now had a picture of Albert locked securely in his mind.

A few weeks later, on a hot Saturday afternoon in July, Burke and another outstanding Secret Service agent named William Houghton were waiting outside a building on lower Broadway in New York. They had been shadowing a well-known German sympathizer named George Sylvester Viereck.

The streets were almost empty. Office workers in the towering skyscrapers were off for the day or had gone home at noon. It was easy to shadow someone, but not so easy to avoid being seen.

Viereck strode out of the building with a tall, Prussian-looking man carrying a bulging brief case. They walked fast toward the nearest station of the elevated railway, which in those days rattled and rumbled on steel trestles above New York's main avenues.

They hurried up the stairs. The two detectives followed at a discreet distance behind. All four got into the next train.

Viereck and his friend, talking German to each other, sat down on a cross seat in the middle of the car. Burke slipped into a side seat just behind them. The tall German put his brief case on the seat between himself and the car window.

He turned to talk to Viereck. For an instant the sunlight shone on the unknown German's cheek. Burke, sitting behind him, caught a glimpse—but it was enough.

On his cheek the German had two telltale saber scars.

Viereck got off the train at Twenty-third Street,

followed by Houghton, the second Secret Service agent. The tall German stayed aboard. A young woman moved into the empty seat next to him. The German, his brief case still propped against the window, began reading.

When he got to Fiftieth Street, a transfer station for another line, he looked up with a jerk. He saw where he was and ran for the door. In his hurry he left the brief case behind.

Swift as a panther, Burke reached for it and grabbed it.

"Hey, Mister, you left your brief case!" the young woman called to the German.

"No, it belongs to me," Burke said quietly and slipped out of the opposite door of the car. Out of the corner of his eye he could see the frantic German trying to get back, but being stopped by a fat woman who blocked the aisle.

Burke stood for a few moments facing the station wall, hiding the brief case against his chest. He busied himself with lighting a cigar until the German had hurried downstairs. Then Burke, too, walked down to the street.

The German spotted him and ran after him. Burke jumped onto a moving trolley car.

"There's a crazy man running after me," he shouted to the conductor. "He's just made trouble up on the elevated station. Don't let him get on!"

The conductor signaled to the motorman not to stop at the next corner. The German was left behind. Soon Burke could breathe easily again.

In grabbing the stranger's brief case and running off with it, Burke had gone beyond the law. The brief case, after all, was private property. The Secret Service had no warrant for Albert's arrest, and no order from a judge to produce the brief case in court.

But Burke was doing what any alert police officer would have done in those days—especially on an assignment from the President.

The papers in the brief case were important enough to be taken at once to the Secretary of the Treasury, William G. McAdoo. They proved that Dr. Albert was, in truth, the director of German plotting in the United States. McAdoo gave all the documents secretly to Frank Cobb, the editor of *The World,* the New York newspaper which was friendliest to the Wilson Administration.

"You can print any or all of these," said the Secretary, "if you first promise me that you will not tell where you got them." His purpose was to throw a scare into German and all other foreign agents in the United States.

Cobb agreed. Soon *The World* splashed this headline across most of its front page:

HOW GERMANY HAS WORKED IN U.S.
TO SHAPE OPINION, BLOCK THE ALLIES
AND GET MUNITIONS FOR HERSELF,
TOLD IN SECRET AGENTS' LETTERS

The documents showed that Dr. Albert had encouraged American munitions workers to go on strike. He had bought a munitions factory in Bridgeport, Connecticut, just to keep its products from going to Germany's enemies. He had also bought a news service to influence American opinion, and in general had taken advantage of American neutrality to work for Germany. For these and other jobs, he had received a total of twenty-seven million dollars from Berlin.

The British and French, too, were taking advantage of neutrality in other ways. But somehow the German plotting looked more evil and dangerous. This is why the snatching of Dr. Albert's brief case was an event of some importance.

The documents helped to arouse the American public against the Kaiser's Germany. They made the people more willing to prepare for war and, two years later, to fight. Incidentally, they gave the Government priceless information with which to fight German plotters.

And their publication made it certain that all foreign agents in the United States would watch their brief cases in the future!

This was the last time any President used the Secret Service for detective work outside its regular Treasury duties.

Once again, in 1924, the Secret Service cracked a famous case at the direct request of President Coolidge. This was the Teapot Dome scandal in which a member of the Cabinet, Albert B. Fall, was proved to have taken a $100,000 bribe. Fall had taken the bribe so that an oil company could get oil wells that belonged to the government. He later went to prison for it, the only Cabinet member to be disgraced in this way in the entire history of the Republic.

But Fall's bribe was, in part, a Treasury matter because most of the money was paid in Treasury bonds. From that day to this, the Secret Service has left most of the government's detective work to the F.B.I.

The men with the star-shaped badge have been busy enough doing their own jobs.

5
What the
Secret Service Is and Does

Every few months the Secret Service gets a letter from someone volunteering to work as a spy.

"I have studied spy cases ever since I was a boy," one such letter began. "I know the methods. I would like to do this kind of work for my country."

A woman wrote that she was well equipped to work for the Secret Service because she, too, had studied spy stories—"and my friends say that I am beautiful."

Of course all such offers, even from beautiful women, are declined with thanks. The letter writers should have known these facts:

Spying abroad in wartime is in charge of the Army, Navy or Air Force. Gathering information abroad in peacetime is the work of the Central Intelligence Agency and other government departments. Catching spies in the United States is the work of the F.B.I.

The Secret Service is not a "cloak-and-dagger" agency, nor is it a kind of super-police entitled to prowl the United States in search of criminals.

Normal police duties in this country are the work of city, county and state police forces. If criminals cross state lines, these local forces can ask the F.B.I. to help in catching most of them. Only certain kinds of criminals, such as counterfeiters, are the special concern of the Secret Service. It works closely with local police to catch them, whether they cross state lines or not.

The Secret Service is a small and special force to which Congress has given three main tasks.

The first and gravest of them is the constant, unsleeping protection of the President, the members of his immediate family, the President-elect and the Vice-President. The job began soon after the shooting of President McKinley in 1901.

But not until 1906 did Congress get around to voting this task into law and voting money to the Secret Service for Presidential protection. In 1913 Congress extended the work of the Secret Service to include the President-elect, during the few weeks between Election Day and the inauguration.

In 1917, when German agents were loose in this country in the First World War, Congress extended the job still further to include the "immediate family" of the man in the White House. Finally, in 1951, Congress wrote a law that summed up all the duties of the Secret Service for the first time, and added the protection of the Vice-President if he asks for it.

The second main duty of the Secret Service—the one that uses more of its agents' time than any other —is to stop the stealing, forging or copying of government checks and government securities, such as savings bonds.

Every year the government issues almost 400 million checks as salaries, pensions or other payments.

If you are entitled to get one of these checks, it probably will reach you in the mail, in a long government envelope. Inside the envelope you will find an oblong of stiff paper headed, in big Gothic letters, "Treasurer of the United States." Below this will be the amount payable, and then, in typed letters, your name and address.

To get real cash for this piece of paper, or to deposit it into a bank account, you must write your name—your "endorsement"—on the back of it.

But suppose the letter carrier puts your envelope into an unlocked mailbox outside your house. Suppose a criminal comes by, dips into the box and steals your check. Then he may write your name on the back in order to get the money which should have gone to you.

This is check forging, which is becoming one of the commonest forms of crime. It is a serious crime. Whoever is caught at it, and convicted, can be sent to jail for ten years, or fined up to $1,000, or both. If the criminal is underage, he can be sent to the reformatory.

Yet more than 30,000 government checks were forged in a single recent year, and the Secret Service arrested more than 2,800 persons for doing it.

Chief U. E. Baughman told a Congressional committee not long ago:

"The forging of checks is becoming most serious, is one of the most profitable criminal rackets, and is increasing daily."

Almost a third of all the forged checks had been stolen from the mail. This explains why the Secret Service begs the American people, year after year, to make sure that the mailbox is locked—or to be on hand when the letter carrier delivers the mail with the government check in it.

The Secret Service also warns the public: "Know Your Endorser!" If shopkeepers refused to cash government checks for people they didn't know, and if bank cashiers insisted on full identification every time, the check-stealing racket could be broken.

The third main duty of the Secret Service, along with protecting the President and catching check forgers, is tracking down and preventing the counterfeiting—the imitating—of paper money and coins.

This is the most dangerous of all its jobs. It is a war against crafty and sometimes ruthless criminals.

An agent on a counterfeiter's trail must know how to shadow a suspect day and night without being noticed. To get his information, he sometimes has to pose as a criminal himself, and live with men who would not hesitate to kill him if they knew he was a federal agent.

One Secret Service man, posing as a criminal a few years ago, had a hair-raising day and night with a gang of counterfeiters. They took him to their hideout in a lonely farm house far from the nearest town. They thought he was one of them.

In the evening the men sat playing cards in the living room while a woman member of the gang, in the kitchen, was standing in the doorway, eyeing him suspiciously.

"Hey, Pete," she called to the head of the gang, "come here for a minute."

The gang leader got up from the card table and sauntered into the kitchen. She whispered to him:

"That guy over there is a cop. I know he is. He used to be on the Pittsburgh police, and I saw him there." It was true. The agent had once been a police detective in Pittsburgh.

Pete called the agent in.

"Now," he said to the woman, "tell him what you just told me."

"All right," said the woman, looking straight and

hard at the agent. "You're not what you say you are. You're a cop, and you used to work on the Pittsburgh police."

The agent was in desperate danger—all alone, unarmed, in a house full of criminals who might murder him if they knew who he really was. He did not let a flicker of fear show in his eyes. To get out of the trap, he decided to laugh it off.

Like a trained actor, he roared with laughs at the very idea that he might be a police agent. He made such a joke of it that he swept all suspicion away. The next day, on a pretext, he slipped away to town, rounded up help from the local police, and raided the hideout. This time he had enough men and guns to battle it out with the criminals if necessary.

All were arrested and later convicted. Pete, the leader, snarled at the Secret Service man, his former companion:

"We should have bumped you off last night. We could have shot you in the back and buried you in the woods—and nobody would have known. Mister, you're lucky!"

Lucky or not, a Secret Service agent has to take such risks in his everyday work. Sometimes his undercover work brings in a huge harvest of counterfeit money. In Los Angeles, only a year or two ago, an agent posing as a counterfeiter persuaded a printer to sell him a bundle of imitation bills.

The printer was arrested. He told the Secret Service who else had been involved. Agents hurried to a theater where an audience was watching a favorite old comedy called *Charley's Aunt.*

One of them slipped into the wings at the side of the stage. He caught an actor trying to hide two paper bags under the floor boards. The bags contained $9,060 in counterfeit bills.

The actor was arrested. The show was stopped. The audience got its money back at the ticket office.

The courage of one undercover agent helped to convict a total of eighteen men and women in this single money-printing plot. The government captured nearly $400,000 in counterfeit bills which might have fooled and cheated the public.

When a Secret Service man is not shadowing or play-acting in undercover work, he has to do the dull, tedious work of every good detective: the patient work of piecing bits of evidence together, of studying handwriting or plowing through police records to find the criminal.

The war against counterfeiters never ends. Sometimes it requires almost as much nerve and skill and bravery as war itself.

6
The Eyes
Are Looking At You!

When a counterfeiter starts playing his criminal game of copying money, the cards are stacked against him. He may profit for a short time, but he almost always loses in the end. To understand why, you have only to look closely at a dollar bill.

Hold it under an ordinary magnifying glass. Study the face of George Washington, taken from the familiar Gilbert Stuart portrait that hangs in thou-

This picture of former President Truman taken during a parade through the skyscrapers of downtown New York is a particularly good example of the alertness shown by Secret Service men on such occasions. Look at their faces. Each one is ready for any emergency.

Miss Mary Ellen Kane, a secretary in the Protective Research Section of the Secret Service, checks a letter with a file headed "Unusual Salutations." There are 24 classifications for letters of this nature.

U.S. Secret Service, Treasury Departme

above: Secret Service Agents are trained to use many types of firearms.

left: Left: A genuine coin. *Right:* A counterfeit coin. On the good coin, the reading (the corrugated outer edge) is even and distinct. On the bad coin, the ridges are crooked and indistinct. A comparison quickly shows the difference.

These are enlarged pictures of the upper left-hand corners of good and bad $1 bills. The part on top of the diagonal dividing line is from the genuine bill. The part under the line is from the counterfeit. Notice that the fish-net lines around the figure "1" are CLEAR and DISTINCT on the GENUINE. Some of the lines on the COUNTERFEIT are BROKEN, and are NOT clear and distinct. (The lines on actual money are even sharper and clearer than in the pictures in this book, which were made from photo engravings.)

COUNTERFEIT

BAD MONEY
LOOKS BAD

GENUINE

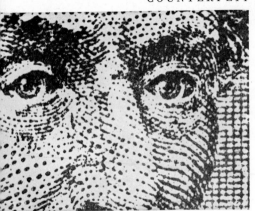

GOOD MONEY
LOOKS GOOD

The photographs on this page are published by special permission of the Chief, U.S. Secret Service, Treasury Department. Further reproduction, in whole or in part, is strictly prohibited.

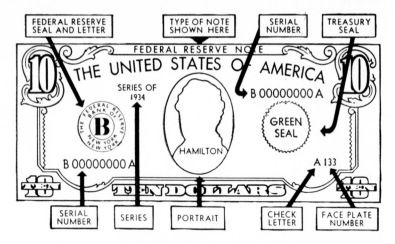

above: This diagram shows the position of important features of paper currency. Study it to *know your money!*

above: Compare! This is an enlarged picture of George Washington, whose likeness is on all $1 bills. It was made from a counterfeit bill and a genuine bill. The portion to the left of the vertical dividing line is from the bad bill. You can easily see the difference. *Published by special permission of the Chief, U.S. Secret Service, Treasury Department. Further reproduction, in whole or in part, is strictly prohibited.*

left: This is an enlargement of part of the Treasury seal on a bad and good $10 bill. The portion at your left is from the counterfeit, that at your right from the genuine. This shows you why the best way to detect a bad bill is to compare it with one you know is good. If you have a bill you think might be counterfeit, crease it through the seal and match it with the opposite half of the seal on a good bill. If the suspected bill is bad, this comparison will help you to detect it. *Published by special permission of the Chief, U.S. Secret Service, Treasury Department. Further reproduction, in whole or in part, is strictly prohibited.*

JEFFERSON

LINCOLN

FRANKLIN

WASHINGTON

HAMILTON

GRANT

JACKSON

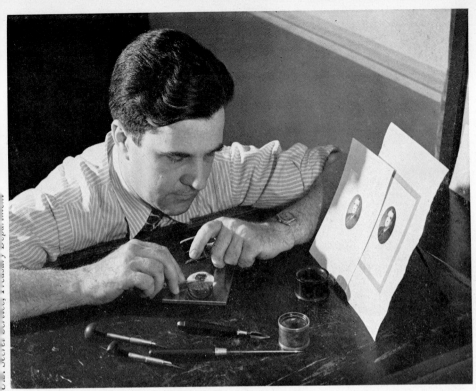

Money engraver at work

When a design for a new note or other security of the Government has been prepared by the Bureau of Engraving and Printing and has been approved by the Secretary of the Treasury, the engravers begin the work of cutting the design in steel. No one engraver does all the work. Each man is a specialist. One works only on portraits, another on lettering, another on scroll work, and so on. No counterfeiter ever has duplicated the artistic work of the expert engravers of the Bureau of Engraving and Printing.

left: YOU SHOULD KNOW THESE FACES

The portraits of these great men appear on United States money. It is important for your protection that you know on which bills these portraits are printed. Particularly you should be familiar with the $1, $2, $5, $10 and $20 bills. All bills of the same denomination bear the same portrait, as follows:

Washington appears on all $1 bills.

Jefferson appears on all $2 bills.

Lincoln appears on all $5 bills.

Hamilton appears on all $10 bills

Jackson appears on all $20 bills.

Grant appears on all $50 bills.

Franklin appears on all $100 bills.

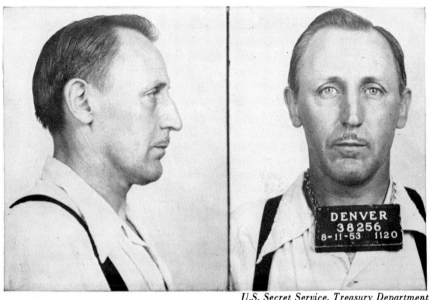

above: Francis L. Henning, counterfeiter of nickels, photographed just after his arrest. His story is told in Chapter 9.

opposite page:

top: Carl Zerse, the music-making money-maker whose story is
told in Chapter 8, photographed just before Secret Service agents
led him away to jail.

bottom: The Denver police took this picture of Donald Roquerre,
the man who changed his fingers (Chapter 10).

A diver for The Philadelphia Police Harbor Patrol recovers a
5¢ die from the Cooper River, Haddonfield, N.J., where Henning
had dumped thousands of counterfeit coins.

This unique bomb carrier was developed by the Secret Service, as told in Chapter 13, to transport explosives with minimum danger to people and property.

The swindle machine described in Chapter 7 and (*inset*) showing sliding compartment.

one made by hand engraving. The white spots on the
eyes are less clear and sharp. The threadlike lines
under the eyes and around the mouth, which give
expression to a portrait, are blurred or broken. The
picture does not have a three-dimensional effect as
it does in a good hand engraving.

So the counterfeiter is up against it if he sets out
to imitate money. If he tries hand engraving, he must
compete with a handful of outstanding craftsmen who
have spent many years in learning and practising
their work. If he tries a short cut with the help of a
camera and a bottle of acid, his imitation cannot possibly be as good as the original.

The portrait, then, is the greatest single protection against people who think they can get rich by
copying money.

But there is a second protection, almost as important as the first. This is the design of paper money:
the decoration around it, the numbers and letters and
seals which appear on it.

As a work of art and design, an American dollar
bill is a horror. No good designer would think of
cluttering up a little piece of paper with so much
lettering and ornament. One of America's greatest
experts on lettering once asked:

"Why can't our money be good-looking? Why can't the numbers and letters be more slender? Why can't there be lots more white space? And why must our money have all those silly curlicues and whirls around the edges?"

The answer, of course, is that our paper money is not intended as a work of art. If it were simple and graceful, like the best of modern design, the counterfeiter would have a far easier time.

Everything on the dollar bill is there for a purpose: either to identify it (every bill has a different number) or to show that it is official (the Treasury seal is there for this reason) or to make it next to impossible for criminals to copy it.

This is why a piece of paper money looks as overstuffed as a room in your great-grandmother's house, where pictures cover every wall and knickknacks every table.

Different engravers work on different parts of the complicated design. Some do the ornamental work, using a geometric lathe, a machine to carve the whirls and scrolls that surround every bill. Some do the lettering, some the numbering, some the Treasury seals.

The scenes of Monticello on the back of the $2

bill, the Lincoln Memorial on the $5, the Treasury on the $10, the White House on the $20, are produced on steel plates by a still different process known as *etching*. They are purposely made intricate with foliage and other details that are hard to copy. No single counterfeiter can possibly do as good a job on all these trimmings as a group of experienced government engravers, each one working on a section of the pattern.

Finally, in addition to the portrait and the design, there is a third protection which has caught hundreds of counterfeiters. This is the special paper used for United States money. Only one factory in the country is allowed to make and sell the special kind of paper on which real money is printed.

The paper is a mixture of half linen and half cotton, with a few bits of red and blue thread in each bill as an added safeguard. It has to be so strong that it can be folded two thousand times without breaking.

Even so, a dollar bill passes from hand to hand so often and is crumpled in so many pockets that it lasts only about nine months. After that time, it is so messy that the banks return it to the Treasury to get a new one.

You would think that no counterfeiter would ever try to make money—with so many handicaps and with the Secret Service waiting to put him behind the bars. Yet the wonder is that so many criminals still do it.

In one recent year alone, the Secret Service arrested 166 counterfeiters, seized eighteen factories making counterfeit notes, and captured $445,044 in bad money before any of it could be passed off on the public as real.

Of the bad money that did go into circulation for a time, $73,041 of it got back into the alert hands of Secret Service agents.

7

A Mean and Sneaking Crime

Why does a counterfeiter do it? What goes on in his mind?

His motive, of course, is greed for money. He wants to "get rich quick." The same motive prompts a holdup man to break into a shop, or a pickpocket to grab a fat wallet when he sees it sticking out of someone's trousers pocket.

Many ordinary thieves commit their crimes on the

spur of the moment or with little planning. The counterfeiter is different. The late Robert H. Jackson, formerly a Justice of the United States Supreme Court, once described the difference in this way:

"Counterfeiting is an offense never committed by accident, nor by ignorance, nor in heat of passion, nor in extremity of poverty.

"It is a crime expertly designed, by one who possesses technical skill and lays out substantial sums for equipment. It is a crime not excused by the fact that 'everyone is doing it.'

"Counterfeiters are few and are not amateur criminals. It is not a crime of courage. It is a sneaking offense, and it cheats small tradesmen and unsuspecting people who have not the skill or experience to detect the imitation."

Long planning, long training and tedious work go into counterfeiting. The criminal has to work for weeks and months in secrecy, where neighbors cannot see him. Therefore, he usually chooses some farmhouse far away from others, or a house surrounded by vacant lots on the edge of a town.

Because his equipment costs money—sometimes thousands of dollars—he usually needs a gang of criminals to finance him. This is why the biggest counterfeit operations are the work of gangs, even though only one man may do the actual engraving.

The gang also needs helpers who will "pass" the bad money—that is, pay it out as if it were real. Passers are paid by shares of the bad money. Usually they are careful to pass only one bill at a time. When the passer offers a counterfeit bill and gets his change in real money, he hurries off to the next town—perhaps to do the same thing again.

Day and night he lives in fear of detection and in hopes that he can escape being caught. His greed is what drives him on.

Since ancient times counterfeiters have been hateful characters. The ancient Greeks had them put to death. The Romans sometimes fed them to the lions. The late Roman emperor Constantine, in the fourth century, ordered them burned alive.

When the great Kublai Khan was emperor of China, at the time of Marco Polo's visit 700 years ago, counterfeiters of paper money had their heads hacked off by a sword.

In seventeenth- and eighteenth-century America, too, colonial governments imposed what may seem to us savage penalties for making imitation coins or paper money. Massachusetts sentenced a Frenchman to stand two hours in the pillory and have both ears cut off for the crime.

Only a few years before the Declaration of Independence, Pennsylvania passed a law sentencing any coin counterfeiter "to the pillory, for the space of one hour, and to have both of his or her ears cut off and nailed to the pillory, and be publicly whipped, on his or her bare back, with twenty-one lashes, well laid on. . . ."

Yet, with all these penalties, counterfeiters had an easier time than nowadays. In Revolutionary days one of the British weapons against the rebellious colonies was copying the paper money issued by the Continental Congress. The imitation money spread so far and wide that the real American money was no longer worth anything. This was one reason why anything without the slightest value was said to be "not worth a Continental."

As the United States grew older, banks were allowed to issue their own paper money in their own designs. (Gradually Congress charged banks more and more for the privilege of issuing such notes, and by 1935 the practice had stopped.) But back in 1893 almost 1,400 banks were entitled to put out money in different designs and in at least ten amounts. With so many kinds of paper money to copy, how could the counterfeiters fail?

The odds against the criminal are far greater today, and he has to be more careful. Sometimes a counterfeiter tries to do the job all alone, without accomplices. This is the most baffling kind of case for the Secret Service because the clues are so few.

One such man walked into a bar in Philadelphia early in this century and ordered a drink. He put a $100 bill on the counter, which was wet where glasses of beer had stood.

"I'm sorry I haven't got anything smaller," he said.

The man behind the bar, picking up the bill, saw that the colors on the wet side of the paper had smudged. A real bill would not do that, for its ink is waterproof.

"I haven't got a hundred dollars' change here," the bartender said. "Wait a minute; I'll run out and get your bill changed."

He ran to a policeman, who arrested the man, took the $100 bill and called the Secret Service to help. The bill, of course, was bad. It was like many others that had bothered the Secret Service in Philadelphia for years.

When the smudged bill was examined under a microscope, as the others had been, the Secret Service found that it hadn't been engraved and printed at all. Every curlicue and whirl around the edges, every letter and number, every threadlike line in the portrait, had been drawn perfectly—by pen and ink!

The man who did it was a laborer who could hardly read or write. He said he had worked a whole week on each bill.

In Secret Service records he is known as the first "Jim the Penman." Not many counterfeiters with costly equipment could have done as well.

Another criminal who tried to outwit the Secret Service posed and dressed as a European nobleman. He moved from city to city, staying at the best hotels, and got hundreds of thousands of dollars by swindling as well as counterfeiting before he was caught. This is how he did it:

In each city he made friends with men who seemed to have plenty of cash in their wallets. At the right time, he dropped his voice to a whisper and said:

"Would you like to make lots of easy money? I'll show you how."

Then he produced a metal box with mysterious-looking buttons, cranks, levers and tiny electric light bulbs on it.

He took a bill from his pocket. "Here is a $20 bill," he said, "I'll copy it right here. I have a piece of plain white paper that's just the size of money. There's a secret chemical inside the box than can transfer this bill to the white paper—and we'll have two $20 bills instead of one."

To demonstrate the process, he put the $20 bill inside the box. He pushed a button, turned a crank and pulled a lever. The electric lights blinked. Something inside the box whirred, and a little drawer flew open. Inside it were, true enough, two $20 bills, one of them brand-new.

"Amazing! But are you sure the new bill is good?"

"Certainly it's good. Take it to any bank if you don't believe me and get it accepted." Of course it was accepted, for the new bill was perfect money.

The swindler's next move was to offer his box for sale. "I'll let you have it," he said, "for five thousand dollars—or, if you'd rather, you can give me the five thousand and I'll make it ten if you give me time."

Usually he got the five thousand, depending on

the wealth of the customer—and quickly moved off to another city.

The purchaser would take the box home and try it. But when the drawer flew open for him, it was empty. By this time the swindler was far away, and another foolish American was poorer by five thousand dollars.

The box, of course, was not a mysterious machine at all. The swindler had simply put two good bills in a hidden section of the box. By turning a crank and pulling a lever he had slid the hidden section into the place where the one $20 bill and the piece of paper had been.

The Secret Service finally caught him because he had been changing the serial numbers on bills, so that each pair of $20 bills in the drawer would look exactly alike, even to the numbering. This was a violation of the anti-counterfeiting laws just as surely as if he had tried to copy an entire bill.

Secret Service men shake their heads sadly about such stories—not because of the swindlers, who are hard to catch, but because so many Americans are still so easily fooled. The agents call this trick "the green goods swindle" because of the green ink used on paper money.

Every year or two some swindler repeats the old trick and still gets away with it—until he lands in prison. In Secret Service offices, old-time agents always remember the saying of P. T. Barnum, the great showman and circus owner:

"There's a sucker born every minute."

8

The Music-Making
Moneymaker

Mrs. Pearl Bridges had a busy morning in her self-service market in DuQuoin, a mining town in southern Illinois. The drawer of her cash register was comfortably filled with bills and change.

Most of the morning customers had gone when a thick-set stranger of about sixty wandered in and rummaged around the shelves. He walked back to Mrs. Bridges' cash counter carrying a 68-cent package of barbecued pork shoulder, a 45-cent chocolate cake and a 19-cent loaf of bread.

He pulled out of his wallet a $10 bill.

Mrs. Bridges rang up the sale. The drawer of her cash register slid open, and she reached for change. But the $10 bill felt greasy. Somehow it wasn't like other bills she had handled that morning. She thought it didn't "feel right."

She stood there fingering it and eyeing her customer. His eyes shifted nervously from her cash register to the door. Without saying anything, she gave him his change. But she was careful to take a good look at him for identifying features: his prominent nose, his sagging chin and the pouches under his blue eyes.

The stranger shuffled out with his parcel. Mrs. Bridges hurried to the door and watched him get into a blue Plymouth parked outside. She wrote down the number of the plate—Illinois 1-005-742.

Then she called the police, who promptly called the nearest field office of the Secret Service, in St. Louis.

The $10 bill was counterfeit, just as Mrs. Bridges suspected. Its workmanship was almost as clear and sharp as that of real money, but there were telltale

marks of the counterfeiter in the rough shading behind Hamilton's head and in the blunt point of the
Treasury seal.

Other bills like it had cheated other shopkeepers
in the area, but no one except Mrs. Bridges had been
alert enough to identify the passer or to note the license number.

The license belonged to Wilmer Trout, a clerk of
the State Highway Department who lived in Nashville, Illinois. To his neighbors in Nashville it was
beyond belief that he could be a counterfeiter, a criminal who copied money. He conducted a real estate
business, was prominent in his church, and was popular enough to have won a nomination for County
Clerk.

But he might be the accomplice. He might lead
the Secret Service to the man who really made the
$10 bills. Day and night, agents watched his house;
several times they followed him to a shabby frame
house on an unpaved street beyond the town. They
saw him talk furtively with the owner. Finally they
decided to pounce on Trout. They obtained a warrant
for his arrest on a charge of possessing and passing
counterfeit money.

One dark night two Secret Service agents followed

Trout as he drove home from a town thirty-nine miles away. The old man was in a hurry. The speed signs on the highway announced a 55-mile limit; but Trout shot ahead at 60, then 65, then 70. The Secret Service car kept up with him like a steel filing attracted to a moving magnet.

On the straight, empty highway, Trout and his pursuers were scorching along at 80 when, far ahead, a red light flashed at a dangerous crossroads. Both cars slowed to a stop. The agents waited until the light turned green. Then they caught up with Trout and forced him to the side of the road.

Agent Elliott Thacker jumped out.

"Don't move—federal agents!" he ordered. "Now take your hands off that wheel and lift them very slowly."

The old man protested but did as he was told.

"I'm agent Thacker of the Secret Service," he went on, "and I have a warrant for your arrest."

The two agents handcuffed him and searched him by the side of the road. In his wallet they found six $10 bills, with exactly the same defects as on the bill paid to Mrs. Bridges in her market. The wallet had a partition in it; on one side were the false bills, on the other $32 in real currency.

"Where did you get those bills?" Agent Vincent Mroz demanded.

"From the bank."

"You're lying, and you know it!"

The agents hustled him back into the car and questioned him again as they drove on.

"Where did you get those bills?"

"From my wife."

"You're still lying!"

They made one more attempt to ask their prisoner for the truth. This time, at last, he gave an answer that was not an evasion. The agents had him locked up for the night in the county jail at Murphysboro. Then they sped away on the trail of the real counterfeiter, the man who made the imitation $10 bills.

Their trail led them the next afternoon into Trout's home town of Nashville. They first borrowed four plainclothes men from the local police force to help them. The six men drove down the unpaved side street to the shabby house where Trout had been seen talking to the owner. The local police jumped out to take up positions around the house, while the agents sprang up the steps and knocked on the door.

A muffled voice, coming as if from far away, called "Come in!"

They opened the door, hands on their pistols in case they needed to use them. An old man, obviously ill, lay in his pajamas on a cot alongside a battered upright piano.

It was hard to tell how old the man was. His face was wrinkled and covered with a stubby growth of beard. His wife, much younger, stood between the agents and the sick man, as if to protect him.

"We are Secret Service agents, and we have a warrant to search your house," Thacker said quietly.

The man on the cot looked at him for a moment with his piercing brown eyes.

"You don't need a search warrant," he said, wheezing with every breath. "I've been expecting you. When I heard Trout didn't come home last night, I was sure he'd been arrested."

"He's in jail," the agent said. "Now, where is it?"

The old man asked his visitors to wait a minute. Instead of answering their question, he climbed out of bed, shuffled over to the piano, and began to play an old song called "Cross My Heart."

"I wrote it myself, long ago," he explained. When

he finished playing, he sank back onto the bed, still panting as if every breath were an effort.

"All right," he said hoarsely. "Go out onto the back porch and you'll find what you are looking for."

The agents found, covered by a tarpaulin, a complete photoengraving plant, including a small printing press, sixteen zinc and copper plates, a camera, ninety-eight negatives and twelve unfinished $10 bills.

Then they came back to question the old man and get his story.

He was Carl Zerse, sixty years old, a former song writer and music publisher. He said he had been studying books on photoengraving in an attempt to rival the workmanship on real money.

"I guess I wanted to do the impossible," he said. "I feel no counterfeiter has done it up to now."

He said he had made 250 $10 bills, "possibly more" (the true figure was nearer 800), and had given Trout eight or ten at a time. He did his work on the back porch at night, keeping his equipment covered in the daytime.

With all the counterfeiting, he still was so short of money that neighbors came bringing him gifts of milk and bread. They never wondered about the metal machinery, covered by a tarpaulin, on the back porch.

But the Secret Service had known something about Zerse. They had watched him for a whole week several months before but could not get enough evidence to arrest him. It was Trout who finally confessed that he had obtained the six counterfeit bills "from Zerse"—which was all the confirmation they needed.

The agents left a local detective to guard Zerse during the night. They returned the next day to take him off to court. They found the old man dressed, in a rumpled white shirt and trousers, but still unshaven.

"May I have a last moment at the piano?" he pleaded. They nodded their permission. Mrs. Zerse had an idea:

"Carl, why don't you play your own song, 'When I Return'?"

"Very appropriate, honey," the old man replied, with a bleak smile. He played, and she sang the words, with tears trickling down her cheeks.

"Do you think I can go on with my music in prison?" he asked the agents. "It will probably be a long time before I touch my own piano—if I ever do it again."

The agents said they could make no promise.

Once more he asked them to wait. As if he were using his last ounce of strength, he pounded the keyboard in the crashing chords of Rachmaninoff's "Prelude in C-sharp Minor." Then the agents led him out of the house and drove him away to East St. Louis, to jail.

Because Zerse was so ill, he was the first of the two to go on trial. He had to be carried into the courtroom on a stretcher. His voice was so feeble that the judge stepped down from the bench and sat alongside the stretcher to hear more clearly. The lawyers, too, huddled around the stretcher.

The old man did not insist on a jury trial; he left the decision to the judge.

"I'm sorry for what has happened, but I told the truth all the way," he whispered. "And I don't intend to do anything wrong again."

He got a two-year sentence "in the custody of the Attorney General of the United States"—meaning that he could be kept in the Federal prison hospital.

Within ten days Zerse was dead—of lung cancer.

His accomplice, Trout, went to trial later. Because of Trout's age and his good reputation among his neighbors, the judge did not send him to jail. Instead, he fined him $2,000 and put him on probation for three years—meaning that he would have to report regularly to the police, and could be jailed at once for any misbehavior.

Trout quickly moved away from Nashville to avoid the anger of his neighbors. He now runs a dry-cleaning business somewhere in the Southwest. He never wants to hear or read the word "counterfeiting" again.

Mrs. Bridges still works behind her cashier's desk, and will never fail to note the license number of anyone whose money doesn't "feel right." Soon after Zerse and Trout were sentenced, she got a letter from the Secret Service thanking her for her "splendid co-operation." With the letter was a check for $100 as a reward.

9
The New Jersey
Nickel Mystery

Most bank cashiers, or tellers, have tiresome jobs. As long as the bank is open to customers, the tellers at the windows must count and hand out money, take in money and count it, for hours on end. After banking hours they count and sort the deposits from big customers, like department stores, and check their accounts until their day's work is done.

But one bank teller never found his job a bore.

He worked in the Pennsauken, New Jersey, National Bank, near Philadelphia. His hobby happened to be coin collecting.

As the nickels and dimes and quarters slipped through his fingers into the till, or cash drawer, they had a special meaning for him. His fingers had the sensitive touch of a craftsman, and his eyes were like magnifying glasses.

One day in 1955 he went to his bank manager with a 1944 Jefferson nickel in his fingers. He held it as if it were a jewel.

"Look at this nickel," he said. "I've never seen one just like it."

"It looks all right to me," the manager said. "What's wrong with it?"

"Look at it through this magnifying glass," the teller persisted. "It hasn't got a little letter 'P' on the back of it, just above the design of Monticello."

The teller was right. American coins come from three government factories, or mints, in Philadelphia, Denver and San Francisco. In wartime, when a special mixture of metals went into nickels, the Philadelphia Mint put its mark, a tiny letter "P" on the back of Jefferson nickels from 1942 through 1945.

"Either there's been a mistake at the Mint, or it's a bad coin," the teller went on. "If it was a mistake, it's a collector's item, and this nickel is worth real money. If it's bad, I think we ought to tell the Secret Service."

The bank asked the Secret Service for its opinion. A few other coin collectors in the Philadelphia area wrote to say that they, too, had spotted Jefferson nickels without the "P." One coin dealer said he would like to get other specimens, because he could sell each one for as much as $1.25.

The Secret Service was puzzled. It had caught plenty of counterfeiters making fifty-cent pieces. But—a nickel?

"I don't believe it," one young agent said as he studied the bank teller's coin. "Why should anyone try to counterfeit a nickel? What can you buy with a nickel anyway? A newspaper, a pack of gum, maybe a small ice-cream cone. Why go to all the trouble of making them?"

But old-timers in the Secret Service remembered that the three mints issue 200 million new nickels every year. If a counterfeiter made vast quantities of them, he just might make a profit. The Secret

Service sent the specimen to the mint in Philadelphia for examination.

The odd-looking nickel was not a mistake. It was counterfeit.

Not only was the letter "P" missing, but there was a flaw in the vertical stroke of the letter "R" in the word "PLURIBUS." The other specimens turned in by coin collectors had the same flaws. Otherwise the coins were devilishly clever imitations that would fool almost everyone.

Now the Secret Service was stumped. It wasn't sure what to do next. With so many hundreds of millions of nickels in circulation, how on earth could it spot the bad ones? How could it ever hope to find the odd and unusual criminal who was making them?

The Secret Service alerted banks in the Philadelphia area and then throughout the country. It put an appeal in the coin collectors' magazines, asking for specimens of the 1944 nickels without the "P." The results were worse than disappointing. Only thirty of the bad nickels showed up.

Five months went by. The head of the field office in Philadelphia reported:

"No success thus far in locating the source."

Then, as it almost always does, the "break" came. A new tenant moved into an empty building at Erial, New Jersey, and called the police to come in a hurry.

The police called Secret Service agents who were astounded at what they saw. On the first floor were punch presses and other coin-making machines that must have cost thousands of dollars. Strewn around the floor, and stored in cupboards, were 67,-950 nickel-sized slugs, like coins without markings on them.

While one of the machines was being carted away, nine finished nickels fell out—all of 1944, and all lacking the tiny letter "P."

This, then, was where the mysterious nickels had come from! A bank deposit slip found in the building showed that a man named Francis Leroy Henning had been depositing as many as $61 worth of nickels at a time in various Philadelphia banks. Along with his equipment he had left a supply of official-looking coin wrappers, showing that he had deposited the nickels in rolls of $2 each.

The Secret Service went into a flurry of detective work to find Henning. It took more than a month of chasing clues, from Baltimore to Cleveland, to catch him. They arrested him in Cleveland and found excellent equipment for counterfeiting $5 bills in his room.

The nickels still interested the Secret Service more than the paper money. After all, a man who would counterfeit a humble nickel was someone very special in the ranks of criminals. How many nickels had he made? And what had he done with them?

"When I knew you were after me," Henning said, "I dumped thousands of the finished nickels into the Cooper River at Haddonfield, New Jersey."

To test his story, the Secret Service drove him to Haddonfield. Henning was a polite, soft-spoken, well-dressed man of sixty-two, and gave no trouble. Willingly, almost eagerly, he pointed to the spot where, he said, he had thrown buckets full of nickels into the water.

Police in a rowboat splashed around for four hours, using a magnet attached to a rope, but could not find a single bucket or coin on the river bottom.

The next day a diver of the Philadelphia Harbor Patrol slithered into the muddy stream. A bomb disposal squad of soldiers from Fort Dix helped by searching the bottom with electronic mine detection equipment. By nightfall they had recovered 14,000 nickels embedded in the mud, and enough counterfeiting equipment to send Henning to jail.

Why he did it was still a mystery and is to this day. Henning had served three years in jail many years ago for counterfeiting $1 bills. But he could have earned much more by honest work than by a bizarre crime. One of his former supervisors said he was "a very talented engineer." Before he started counterfeiting nickels he was earning $1,000 a month in an engineering firm.

He told the Secret Service of various machines he had designed and ordered made for him. One was a metal stamping machine with a pressure of 250,-000 pounds. Another was a blast furnace capable, he said, of producing 3,200 degrees of heat— enough to melt silver and other metals that coins are made of.

He paid $6,800 for sheets of cupro-nickel, from which nickel coins are made, after making a chemical analysis of real nickels to make sure that his imitations would have the same metal content.

Henning insisted that he hadn't intended, at first, to make imitation nickels. He said his machines had cost so much that "counterfeiting became, to my mind, the way out of my financial troubles." Again and again he argued that his machines could do perfectly legal things, although the Secret Service could see no use for them except criminal money-making.

Altogether Henning's equipment cost him $25,-000, or half a million nickels. He never made a nickel of net profit on his coin counterfeiting. Instead, he drew a three-year jail sentence and a fine of $5,000 for part of the expense he had caused the government in catching him. He will have to earn the $5,000 when he comes out of jail.

It all shows that there's something strange about counterfeiters. As Secret Service men will tell you again and again, you must be foolish as well as crooked to go into that kind of business.

10
The Man Who
Changed His Fingers

The ocean called "Pacific" is not always as peaceful as its name. Along the coast of California, storms can whip its waves to fury. Many a ship has come to grief on the jagged rocks offshore. Bits of wrecks and cargoes often float in with the tide, and wanderers on the beaches find such souvenirs of the sea.

One windy Sunday not long ago, a man and his wife were having a beach lunch in a sheltered cove.

The tide was out. In a crevice between two barnacled rocks the woman noticed something shiny in the water. She fished it out and found that is was a new, unopened can of printer's ink.

Near by, on the sand, she picked up something much more curious. It was a bright zinc plate with the design of a $20 bill photoengraved on one side of it.

The picnickers had the good sense to put a marker near the place. Then, instead of taking their trophies home, they reported their find to the Coast Guard at the Pigeon Point lighthouse.

The Coast Guard went to work to search the water's edge. Next day this teletype message reached the Secret Service in Washington:

"Recovered from ocean 3.7 miles north of U. S. Coast Guard Pigeon Point lighthouse yesterday 11 relief-etched plates, two photoengraved plates and various portions of plates for $20 Federal Reserve notes, five-pound hand press and damaged Corona typewriter. As tide receded this A.M. Coast Guard recovered an additional two cartons of materials."

The acting Chief of the Secret Service wired back:

"Thanks. Very good!"

Within twenty-four hours the Secret Service in California sent an alarm to the police of all Western states to stop a green sedan with the California license plate 6U6139. It had a warrant for the arrest of Donald Darling Roquerre.

This is Roquerre's story.

Roquerre wasn't his real name at all. He was born Albert Snead. When he was twelve, his mother died, leaving him to shift among relatives who didn't want him. He never got beyond the fourth grade in school.

He was a moody boy, sometimes cruel to animals, often mean to other children. Of all the things that made him unhappy, his name irritated him the most. He thought it wasn't romantic enough.

So when he grew up, he changed it to "Donald Darling Roquerre" and felt he could face the world with better prospects. He always was a boy who liked deceptions. He wanted to be someone he wasn't—someone dashing, rich and famous. In fact, he was just a truck driver.

When he was a young man, almost twenty-five years ago, he stole a truck and drove it across a state line. This brought him a three-year term in prison. After serving his time, he wanted a new job as a truck driver in Newark, New Jersey.

But to get a license there, he would have to be fingerprinted. And since his fingerprints were already on the police records, his criminal past would become known, and he would not get the job.

Wondering how he could hide his past, he had a gruesome idea. He had read in a detective story magazine about a criminal who had changed his fingerprints by having a doctor operate on him. Why not do it? And why bother to use a doctor?

One night, in his shabby room, he began work on his right ring finger and his right middle finger. He wrapped rubber bands tightly below the tips to shut off circulation of blood. When the fingers had become blue, he took a safety razor blade and sliced off tiny pieces of skin about a quarter of an inch square. It hurt very little at the time because the fingertips were as numb as if they had been frozen.

Then he transposed the skin, wrapping each fingertip with thread and each whole finger in gauze. At the end of a month he had done the whole grim job on eight fingers.

Now he could fool the police! Now, he thought,

nobody could know that he had once served time in jail.

For almost twenty years he stayed out of trouble. But nothing went right for him. He married, but not happily. He ran a filling station in California; the business failed.

"How are we going to get back on our feet?" his wife asked him one evening.

Roquerre, moody as always, came up with another deception.

"We could pass bad checks," he suggested. "You know, print some checks on a big company, make them out to ourselves, and get them cashed. Then we'd be back on our feet. I'd even counterfeit money —if I knew how to do it."

His wife did not like the plan, but Roquerre went ahead with it. In his home town of Santa Cruz, California, he took lessons in photoengraving for two months. At various places up and down the Pacific Coast he bought materials for printing and counterfeiting.

A boarded-up part of his basement became his secret workshop. He succeeded in forging forty checks on an insurance company and twenty-five on the Southern Pacific Railway Company, and got

enough cash from them to buy still more counterfeiting and forging equipment.

One summer weekend in 1955 a Santa Cruz detective knocked on the door of the Roquerres' house.

"Where's your husband?" he asked Mrs. Roquerre.

"He's away—I don't know where he is. I haven't
seen him for a long time," she answered. "Why do
you want my husband?"

"Because," the detective said, "we're looking for
someone who's been forging Southern Pacific checks.
We think his name is Don D. Roquerre."

The detective went away and questioned others
in Santa Cruz, including the owner of the local
photoengraving shop. That night the Roquerres
hurriedly loaded metal plates, a hand press, cans of
ink and a Corona typewriter into their car, and
dumped everything into the Pacific about three
miles north of Pigeon Point lighthouse.

Then they made their getaway, driving south on
the coastal highway.

Within forty-eight hours, the Coast Guard fished
their counterfeiting equipment out of the water. It
was the "break" in a case that had stumped the
Secret Service for weeks. The typewriter could still

write after two days in the sea; its letters were iden-
tical with those on the forged railway checks.

What was more, the Secret Service knew the license number of Roquerre's car. An alert detective
in Los Angeles had seen a woman, after cashing a
false check, dash away in a green sedan with the
California license 6U6139. The car was registered
in the name of Don D. Roquerre of Santa Cruz.

Now Roquerre was in trouble, wherever he might
be.

Secret Service agents and local police, armed
with a search warrant, hurried to the house in Santa
Cruz. Nobody was at home. They broke in the door.
They knocked down a wooden wall in the basement.
Behind it they found a printing press and other
heavy machinery for counterfeiting money.

The alarm went out by radio and teletype. In
southern California, in Arizona and New Mexico, in
western Texas, police eyed the license plates of
green sedans on the highway. The Secret Service
finally caught the Roquerres in a motel outside
Denver. Their car, near by, sagged with the weight
of paper, ink, enamel, nitric acid and other counterfeiting material packed into it.

Roquerre, cool and calm, insisted there had been

"some mistake." As he was being handcuffed, his wife said:

"Well, it's a relief to have the suspense over."

He got a five-year sentence for forging and counterfeiting; she went to jail for an indefinite term of six months to fourteen years for check forging. Not long afterward, prison officials had to move Roquerre to a Federal medical center because his mind had snapped. He had terrifying dreams and visions that people were trying to cut off his fingers.

What about the double fingerprints? Why had they not thrown the police and Secret Service off the trail? The answer is a story in itself. Years before, Roquerre had been fingerprinted during a census of all ex-convicts in Los Angeles. He didn't worry; he gave a false name. But alert experts of the F.B.I. matched the two sets of prints—the first, taken when he was a young criminal, and the second, after he had mutilated his fingers—and had filed both under the name of Roquerre.

When the Secret Service got the warrant to arrest him, it asked the F.B.I., in the normal way, to supply his fingerprints. The F.B.I. has prints of everyone who has served time in jail, and makes them available to the Secret Service or to state or local police. In Roquerre's case, it sent not one set of prints, but two—with a complete explanation.

By operating on his fingers, Roquerre had done the very opposite of hiding his past. His second fingerprints had indelible white scars in the places where he had grafted the bits of skin. Far from fooling anyone, he had advertised his past as surely as if he had worn a sign saying:

"I am Don Roquerre. I am a dangerous criminal!"

11
How to Tell
Good Money from Bad

The Secret Service used to be truly secret in its methods of catching counterfeiters. Its agents seldom, if ever, explained their work to the newspapers or the public, or to anyone except the proper committees of Congress—in strictly private session.

But in the nineteen thirties the secrecy began to backfire. It actually helped counterfeiters to fool the public. It kept the American people in the dark about the differences between good money and bad.

The Chief of the Secret Service, then Frank J. Wilson, was so troubled that he asked for a meeting with his superior officer at the Treasury, Assistant Secretary Herbert E. Gaston. Gaston had been a brave and brilliant newspaper editor before going to the Treasury.

"We're just not getting ahead of the counterfeiters," the Chief told him. "We catch them all the time, but more of them seem to pop up all the time too.

"I think we have to try something brand-new —something the Secret Service has never done before."

Gaston was a man who liked to try new methods.

"Good!" he said. "Now tell me what you've got in mind."

"We have to go right to the public and teach them how to know their money," the Chief answered. "I'd like to see the Secret Service go to bank tellers, shopkeepers, school children, anyone who might be fooled by a counterfeiter, and get them to help us.

"We'll have to tell them things that we've always

kept to ourselves. But it will be worth it—if we
can get millions of people to recognize bad money
when they see it."

Many old Treasury officials, and veteran Secret
Service agents, were horrified. But Gaston liked the
idea, and so did the Secretary of the Treasury in
those years, Henry Morgenthau, Jr. After all, they
argued, the government of a free country must have
the people's help and understanding in fighting a
war against a foreign enemy.

Why, then, shouldn't it do the same in a war
against criminals?

This was the start of the "Know Your Money"
campaign which the Treasury launched in 1937. It
was a revolution in Secret Service methods. Chief
Wilson ordered agents off their regular duties to
talk to citizens' groups all over the country. Movies
and pamphlets taught millions how to spot bad
money. Warning notices went up on cash registers,
telling cashiers what to do if someone turned in a
bad bill.

Now the counterfeiter could not fool all the
people. He soon discovered that the people were
aware of his tricks and were on the lookout for

them. It was almost as if the Secret Service, with its tiny force of 300 men, had become an army of millions.

The advice that went to the American public then is just as good today. Anyone can follow it, even without a magnifying glass. Here it is:

How to Detect Counterfeit Bills

1. Know your money! Study the bills you receive, so as to become familiar with the workmanship on them, especially in the portraits.

2. Compare a suspected bill with a genuine of the same type and amount. Observe these things:

Portrait:

On a *counterfeit* bill, it is dull, smudgy, or unnaturally white, scratchy. The oval background is dark, the lines are irregular and broken. The portrait merges into the background.

On a *genuine* bill, the portrait stands out distinctly from the oval background. The eyes appear lifelike. The background is a fine screen of regular lines.

Colored Seals:

On a *counterfeit* bill, the saw-tooth points around the rim of the seal are usually uneven, broken off.

On a *genuine* bill, the saw-tooth points around the rim are even and sharp.

Serial Numbers:

On a *counterfeit* bill, the figures are poorly printed, badly spaced, uneven in appearance.

On a *genuine* bill, the figures are firmly and evenly printed, and well spaced.

Paper:

A *counterfeit* bill generally has no colored threads, but these may be imitated by very small red and blue ink lines.

Genuine bills are printed on distinctive paper in which very small red and blue threads are scattered. The threads are not always noticeable on bills that are badly soiled or worn.

3. Rubbing a bill on a piece of paper will *not* prove it is genuine or counterfeit; ink can be rubbed from good bills as well as bad ones.

4. Consult an experienced money handler or police officer to make sure, if you are still in doubt, whether a bill is genuine or counterfeit.

5. Remember, not all strangers are counterfeiters, but all counterfeiters are likely to be strangers.

The Secret Service also told the public how to detect counterfeit coins. Here is some of its advice:

How to Detect Counterfeit Coins

1. Drop coins on a hard surface. Genuine coins have a bell-like ring; most counterfeit coins sound dull.

2. Feel all coins. Most counterfeit coins feel greasy. Compare questionable coins with known genuine coins of the same amount.

3. The tiny parallel carvings, or "reeding," on the outer edge of genuine coins are even and regular. The reeding on the edge of counterfeit coins is uneven, crooked or missing in parts. Only silver coins have reeded edges; pennies and nickels have smooth edges.

By its continuing "Know Your Money" campaign, the Secret Service has taken the American people into its confidence. But the law still bristles with penalties for doing anything that might help a counterfeiter.

You can be sent to prison for fifteen years for photographing or printing any picture of American paper money, like those in this book, without official permission.

It is illegal to draw or print a picture that imitates paper money on a card or advertisement. It is illegal to make or sell or give away any ornament or gadget that looks like an American or foreign coin.

In recent years, the laws relating to counterfeiting have been made less strict in two small ways. Now it is perfectly legal to photograph coins or print pictures of them. It is legal, too, to print black-and-white photographs of postage stamps—but pictures of United States stamps must be less than three-fourths the size of the real stamps, or more than one and a half times the real size. And they can be used only for philatelic purposes in articles, books or circulars intended for stamp collectors.

The Secret Service is still strict—some people

think it is over-strict—in interpreting the laws against counterfeiting. For example, you never see real money shown on television or in the movies, or in a play at the theater. As if a counterfeiter could learn anything by seeing a $20 bill flashed onto a television screen! He probably has plenty of real bills to study whenever he wants to. But if there is a film, there is a negative; and a negative can be used to make a plate.

On the floor of the Treasury office of Robert F. Grube, the agent in charge of the Counterfeit Section, is a Turkish rug six feet long, two feet wide and half an inch thick, patterned on an American dollar bill. The Secret Service spotted it long ago in a department store window, and was authorized to seize it as a violation of the law. The rug is 115 times as big as a real dollar bill. How could any counterfeiter possibly get ideas from it?

The Secret Service does not mind looking silly in such matters. Its attitude is:

"The law is the law—and if we permit one imitation, we'll just open the door to others."

At least the Treasury has given up the self-defeating secrecy of the old days. The "Know Your

Money" campaign has done a great deal to help put counterfeiters out of business

Some greedy criminals, of course, will always be foolish enough to try to copy money. New processes of printing and photography may help them for a time—until the Secret Service catches them.

Actually, the Secret Service no longer regards counterfeiting as its most dangerous problem.

When any of the fifty-seven field offices today has a backlog of unsolved cases, and too much work for its agents to handle, it uses a system of "priorities" —of classing one type of case as more vital than others. Nowadays check-forging cases are the least urgent. Counterfeiting cases are a little more so. At the top of the list, always regarded as the most urgent cases of all, are those involving the protection of the President.

12
Why People
Threaten the President

Why should anyone want to kill or harm the man in the White House? The people have elected him for four years. As President he is the personal symbol of his country, whatever his political party may be. Millions who voted against him may dislike what he does as President, but they would not dream of hurting him as a human being.

Yet every year the White House gets more than

15,000 letters, addressed to the President, which call him vile names, threaten to kill him, or just have a "crazy" sound about them. More than a thousand of these are serious enough for the Secret Service to investigate. Other threats, not put into letters, are reported from field offices throughout the country.

The law is clear—and severe—on this subject. Every American has a right to send a letter to the President or to any other public official. He can praise, blame, offer advice or complain. But whoever *threatens* the President or Vice-President in writing—or in talk which anyone else can hear—can be sent to jail for five years.

Why, then, do the newspapers report so few arrests for this crime? The answer is that 99 out of 100 of those who threaten the President are mentally ill. Instead of being arrested and tried as criminals, they are led away tactfully for questioning by a mental doctor. Some are so ill that they are dangerous, and have to be shut way in mental hospitals where they can be treated and prevented from harming others.

Nobody can understand the problem of protecting the President without remembering these sad and dreadful facts:

Almost seven million cases of mental illness in the United States have been reported by hospitals or private doctors.

Millions more are unreported; that is, they walk the streets and do their jobs and seem to be living normal lives. But at night, brooding and thinking twisted thoughts, they may sit down and write an unsigned letter or postcard threatening to kill the President.

There is no more disgrace in having such mental illness than in having measles or whooping cough. The 700,000 people in mental hospitals in the United States are there, as a rule, simply because they have found the pressures of the world too great for them. To the rest of us, who call ourselves "normal," all the mentally ill are pathetic people, like those who are sick in any other way.

But to the Secret Service they are more than pathetic. Mental illness is the Number One problem of the Secret Service in its solemn duty of protecting the President.

"Not all the mentally ill are dangerous," says Dr. Winfred Overholser, who directs St. Elizabeths, the government's huge mental hospital in Washington.

"But it's never safe to assume that none of the mentally ill is dangerous."

The Secret Service can take no chances. It has to delve into the dark shadows of diseased minds. Its agents must understand and recognize the different forms of mental illness, especially the kind that may lead to a White House tragedy. They have to follow up each threat, no matter how "crazy" it sounds— because a man who says he will kill the President may really do it if he gets the chance.

What kind of people are these? What makes them do it? Listen to Dr. Jay Hoffman, who has treated scores of them at St. Elizabeths and has studied their records:

"These patients are, in general, a pitiful lot. Most of them have had poor jobs and never were able to hold a job for long. Most are unhappily married or unmarried, deprived of family life.

"The theme you find in their life histories again and again is that of loneliness, frustration, failure. They are the 'Sad Sacks' of the community."

Being a "Sad Sack," such a person often tries to make up for his sense of failure by imagining that he is someone grand and powerful—maybe a General of the Army, maybe the Chief Justice, maybe even the President.

He really believes it. He can't stand the world as it exists. He has moved from the world of reality into the world of dreams, or, as the doctors say, of "delusions." Of course such people are mentally ill and need treatment.

One poor sharecropper in Kansas said he heard voices telling him that he was the next President. He hitchhiked all the way to Washington and showed up at the White House gate, saying:

"Here I am!"

Another said he was God.

"How do you know?" the policeman asked him politely.

"Because I can direct cars in traffic."

"But how does that make you God?"

"Well, the cars don't hit me when I cross the street—so I'm sure I'm God."

Still another, living in his world of dreams, identified himself by saying he was very, very important.

"God is Number One," he said, "Jesus Christ is Number Two, and I am Number Three."

At another stage of their mental illness, many of these pitiful people decide that someone is persecuting them. The family, the community, the government or the whole world is "against" them—trying to poison them, rob them, or take away the fame and fortune they think is theirs.

The Secret Service is especially alert to watch anyone with such a grievance if he directs it at the President. For such a person may well decide to do something about it—usually with a pistol.

Booth had a burning grievance when he killed Lincoln; so did Guiteau when he shot Garfield, and Czolgosz when he fired through his handkerchief at McKinley. By present-day standards all of them would have been sent away to mental institutions.

Dr. Hoffman, at St. Elizabeths, finds it odd that these people who feel themselves so grand, or so badly treated, seldom complain against being in a mental hospital.

"Most of them," he says, "are quiet, pleasant, congenial, co-operative, well-behaved." Yet at St. Elizabeths many of the so-called "White House cases" are considered among the most dangerous patients of all. These people live in a building surrounded by a twenty-foot wall. Inside the wall are garden plots where they can get outdoor exercise and do a little farming. But nobody inside the wall, not even the guards, has a key to get out. When they are ready to leave, they signal another guard outside the gate.

The Secret Service has its own term for the sickness of those who threaten the President: "the Presidential complex." It does not matter who the President is. Many of these mentally disturbed men and women have written to Presidents Roosevelt, Truman and Eisenhower alike, announcing to each:

"I am going to kill you."

Since a letter writer may have a grievance against all society, he naturally writes to the President who is in many ways the head man of American society. Some write asking for money, for advice, for relief from those they think are "against them."

And when they threaten, they are honest about it. They see nothing peculiar or wrong about wanting to kill the President; therefore, they do not usually lie about their plans.

During the Second World War a man came to Washington from Detroit, imagining that if he got attention he would get a better job. He decided that a wonderful way to get attention was to shoot President Roosevelt.

For two weeks he lay in wait in Lafayette Park, just across the street from the front of the White

House. He thought the President would come and go by the front entrance (which Mr. Roosevelt almost never did). The man had a submachine gun which he hid at night in the shrubbery.

One day he decided to wait no longer. He strode quickly across the street toward the White House— so quickly that he crossed against a red light. A traffic policeman on the corner blew a whistle and ordered him back to the curb.

The man was furious at being stopped.

"You can't do this to me," he snapped at the policeman. "I've come on important business."

"And what's so important about your business?"

"I've come here to shoot the President!"

Of course he was taken to the police station for questioning and later to a mental home.

Until about 1940 the Secret Service simply tried to keep such "cranks" away from the White House, and provided a bodyguard for the President at all times. Not until 1940 did it find a way to prevent most of these deluded people from even coming to Washington. In that year the Secret Service devised a brand-new system which probably has done more to protect the President than all the bodyguards of fifty years.

13
Fifteen Thousand
Threats on File

There's nothing on the door except "Room 98."

The tourists who flock to Washington never see it, tucked away on the ground floor of a building just across a narrow street from the White House.

But this is a room of some importance to the American people. It is one of the nerve centers of the Secret Service in its unending work of protecting the President from harm.

Twice a day a White House messenger brings to Room 98 a bundle of twenty or thirty letters, all addressed to the President. Someone on the White House staff has already opened each letter and attached the envelope to it. A few letters reach Room 98 in cellophane wrappers with red tabs showing the name of the secretary who has opened them.

All are the day-to-day harvest containing the threats, the vile names, the rambling discussion of grievances, which suggest that someone with "the Presidential complex" is at work.

The White House staff has been trained for years to sort out these letters and rush them to the Secret Service. Those with the most direct threats, or the most violent language, are in cellophane to preserve any fingerprints.

For more than seventeen years, agents in Room 98 have been studying, cross-indexing, photographing and filing evil letters addressed to the President. By now the file contains at least fifteen thousand direct and veiled threats, and perhaps a hundred thousand other letters from mentally unbalanced writers who might, someday, become dangerous.

In the entire field of crime prevention there is

nothing quite like this library of threats and the system by which the Secret Service uses it.

What happens when a Secret Service agent begins studying one of these letters? His first job is to fill out an "analysis sheet" on which he must answer twenty-four different questions.

The signature? There is none on the letter he is examining. It doesn't matter, because few such correspondents dare to sign their true names.

The Secret Service man notes the Los Angeles postmark.

The handwriting slants so heavily that the script letters seem almost to be lying on their sides. The agent notes this carefully.

The "E" in the script is not a loop, as in ordinary writing, but is three-pronged as in capital letters. The agent notes this too.

The salutation and the address on the envelope spell the President's name "Eisenhaur." The letter calls him "a dirty Communist." It talks vaguely about "my six-shooter."

To a good Secret Service man, all these and other peculiar features are clues, just as surely as a cleft chin or a scar on a cheek. They are the keys with which the Secret Service can unlock the identity of a nameless letter writer thousands of miles away.

A secretary takes the answers from the analysis sheet and writes them, one by one, on twenty-four cards labeled "spelling," "postmark," "handwriting," and so on. Now the agent starts searching a huge file of drawers which covers an entire wall of the office next to Room 98.

He looks first in a card-drawer labeled "spelling" to see whether any previous letter writer has spelled the name "Eisenhaur." He goes to another set of drawers and searches past the A's and B's in the cards to a section in the C's labeled "Communist." He is looking for another letter that calls the President a "dirty Communist."

The work is tedious but not too hard. Within half an hour the card index has told him that there are three previous letters from Los Angeles, all in the same slanting handwriting with the three-pronged "E."

One of the three spelled it "Eisenhaur." Two others, written years ago, were addressed to Presidents Roosevelt and Truman, and each one call him a "dirty Communist." The same number indexes all three.

With this information, the agent opens a big

drawer at the bottom of the wall and pulls out a yellow folder. Inside it are not only the three actual letters, in cellophane wrappers, but also the name, address and photograph of the man in Los Angeles who wrote them.

The Secret Service had tracked him down long ago. He had gone to a mental hospital and been let out in 1953 because he seemed to be recovered.

"Here's one who's at it again," the agent reports to Joseph J. Ellis, Jr., his supervisor in Room 98.

"Contact the field office," Mr. Ellis asks, "and tell them I want a report."

A teletype message speeds to the Los Angeles field office. An agent on duty there interrupts his work on a counterfeiting case and hurries to the letter writer's address. Soon the writer is back in the mental hospital where he had spent so much time, and the authorities have promised to let the Secret Service know in advance if and when he is ready for release again.

Sometimes, of course, a letter writer is not so obliging about giving clues. He may think he can hide his identity if he types his threat on plain white paper.

Like so many others who think they can outwit the Secret Service, he is wrong.

Every typewriter is numbered, and the shop that sold it usually has a record of the purchaser. Whether the machine is new or old, its writing usually has some defect which an expert can spot under a microscope. As for paper, every sheet can be analyzed, traced to the manufacturer and often to the shop where it was sold.

Because so many write to the President again and again, and because the file has grown so big and well organized, the Secret Service can match more than nine out of ten new letters with others already in the drawers. If a writer has been in a mental hospital or prison, agents file his photograph along with his record and copies of his letters, just in case he repeats the offense.

Naturally the Secret Service cannot match all letters in this way. The new ones often require patient detective work. Sometimes the writers go untraced for months or years. The least dangerous are the ones that give the Secret Service the most trouble in finding them.

"It's a thankless job," says Mr. Ellis as he plows through the day's mail, "because so much of what we do is to prevent something from happening."

But the President and those around him are grateful, and the whole country ought to be. For if this system of "protective research" had existed in the last century, at least two Presidential murderers probably would have been caught long before committing their crimes.

Booth, who killed Lincoln, certainly would have been watched and caught if there had been a Secret Service and a law against threatening the President. Field offices would have told the Washington headquarters about Booth's wild speeches in which he talked openly about murdering Lincoln.

Guiteau, the busybody who killed Garfield, was another. His letters to Garfield surely would have found their way to Room 98 and its filing cases. For Guiteau had a perfect case of the "Presidential complex." He was an obvious man to watch—if anybody in the government had bothered about such men in those days.

As for Czolgosz, who killed McKinley, he was not a letter writer, and Room 98 might not have known about him in advance. But the Secret Service never would have let this man file past the President with a hand wrapped in a bandage. Today it has an ironclad rule that nobody with bandaged hands or arms, or crutches, can get near the President, even at the most formal White House reception, without having been checked in advance.

Not all the work of Room 98 is the analysis of letters. Through its field offices in fifty-seven cities, the Secret Service keeps in touch with about two thousand "active cases." That is, agents throughout the country pay regular visits to some of the former letter writers, keep track of their changes of address, and report on them to Washington.

In another location is the White House mail room, where all letters and packages addressed to the President are examined by x-ray and other devices before delivery to the White House. Sometimes the supervisor of Room 98 gets a hurry call by telephone from the mail room:

"Can you come over right away to look at a parcel?"

Mr. Ellis loses no time in getting there. The package might contain one of many kinds of explosive contraptions. If there is any suspicion about it, one man, and only one, carries the package to the nearby courtyard, and puts it into one of the oddest-looking vehicles in America.

This is a truck so strongly built that a bomb could explode inside it without doing serious damage. Its body is a cylinder of coiled steel cables; the driver on the front seat is protected against flying fragments by a sloping sheet of armor plate.

When one of these trucks was new, the Secret Service tested it by exploding fourteen sticks of dynamite inside it. Nothing happened to the driver; the only damage to the truck was one punctured tire.

All the same, the truck carries one big sign on each side and another at the rear, warning the public:

DANGER

EXPLOSIVES

Keep Away

Once the suspicious parcel is inside, fastened tightly against slipping or bumping, the truck hurries off by a carefully planned route to an open field on the edge of Washington. Here long tongs, hooked on from the outside, pull the package apart—and sometimes explode it—without risk.

Out of the White House police force of 154 men, twenty-four have volunteered to do this possibly dangerous duty with the bomb carrier, day or night. After all, the men of the Secret Service know they must be "prepared to sacrifice their lives, if necessary, in protection of the President."

14
The Mystery Man
on Pier 59

Tugboats hoot and whistle all day and night off **Pier 59**, which juts into the busy Hudson River in New York.

The pier is never still. The work of loading freight goes on even at night, when the city is dark and sleeping. In offices on the second floor of the pier, dozens of typewriters click away, late into the night, as shipping clerks struggle to fill out the forms needed for every voyage.

In the daytime the pier echoes to the rattle of winches, the shouts of longshoremen, the scurrying of porters and passengers, whenever a great ship slides alongside or sails for far places with hundreds aboard.

In this clatter of noise and confusion, a Secret Service agent walked quietly and coolly up and down the pier several years ago. He did not notice the crowds, nor would they have paid particular attention to him. He was intent on inspecting every little office on the pier: one where the shipping company's clerks take passengers' tickets, another where Customs men study the declarations of incoming travelers, still another where the chief porter gives assignments to his men.

He was there on a grim errand—to save the life of the President of the United States.

The White House had received an unusually vicious letter. It did not directly threaten to kill the President; but it was so violent in tone, it called him by so many evil names, that the Secret Service knew it had to catch the writer without delay.

"This one could be a killer," the agents in Washington agreed as they read and studied the letter. A man who could write such things might easily carry his violence to the shooting stage.

The letter was signed "Peter Hayward," but this was not necessarily a clue. Writers of such letters usually are ashamed and afraid to sign their real names. The postmark was Brooklyn, New York, but this, too, was of little help, for Brooklyn has more than three million people.

The Secret Service did, however, have two clues. First, the letter was typewritten. By examining its typed letters under a microscope, agents discovered that the letter was written on an L.C. Smith machine. Apparently the machine was old and battered because its letters were no longer straight and even.

Second, and more important, was a return address on the envelope: "Pier 59, Hudson River, New York." This, clearly, was the first place to look for the man who might be an assassin.

A teletype message from Washington clacked onto the receiver in the New York field office of the Secret Service. Agent John Hanly, a first-class investigator, hurried to Pier 59 to begin his search.

He discovered that all the typewriters on the pier were in the offices of the shipping company on the upper deck. There were forty typewriters of different makes. But in one room, the office of the port steward who orders food and other supplies for the ships, he found twelve L.C. Smith machines.

Patiently, politely, without disturbing the typists more than necessary, Hanly got samples of the type-writing from all of them. With the permission of the company, he posed as a mechanic.

"I've come from the typewriter company," he would explain. "Would you mind if I tried your machine to see if it's all right?"

Hanly hurried back to his own office to examine the results. He matched each specimen against a vastly enlarged photograph of the original typing.

One of them matched exactly! It had come from a battered L.C. Smith machine, and it had the same uneven typing as the vicious letter that had reached the White House.

Late at night, when the clerks were not working, Hanly went back to the pier and to the typewriter desk at which the letter writer had worked. In the drawers he found sheets of white paper and envelopes. They, too, exactly matched those of the White House letter.

The next morning Hanly was ready to pounce. The

clues all pointed to a sixty-year-old shipping clerk named John Enrico.

"It can't be true!" the office manager said. "Everyone likes this man. He's polite, reliable, sober. He couldn't possibly have written a thing like that."

Hanly sent for the old man anyway.

"Did you write this letter?"

The clerk looked at it quickly, flushed and said: "Yes, I did—but I'm sorry I wrote it." He said he had been "upset" because President Truman had dismissed General Douglas MacArthur from Far Eastern commands in 1951. Enrico was a veteran of the First World War.

"All right, Mr. Enrico," said Hanly. "Please come with me. We're going to the Secret Service office at 90 Church Street. We'll want to ask you some questions."

Because Enrico had a family that could be responsible for him, because he had a good record with no previous offense or mental illness, the Secret Service and the United States Attorney decided to let him off with a warning. His name and address, and his original letter, will stay in the files just in case he writes another such letter—but he has not done so in the past six years.

A more difficult case for the Secret Service, and one more dangerous, was that of a man who wrote half a dozen foul letters to the President from New York and other cities. Instead of signing just any false name, this reckless letter writer "signed" the names of prominent men and women.

The handwriting was the same on all of them. It matched the writing of an earlier letter writer who had once fought with a New York policeman while resisting arrest.

But it was hard to find this man. The Secret Service might never have caught him if the letter writer had not also "signed," as one of his prominent names, "Stephen Kennedy, Police Commissioner, New York City."

When an agent showed him this letter, Commissioner Kennedy was outraged that anyone should have dared to use his name in such a way.

"I'm going to assign one of my best detectives to you as long as you need him to catch this fellow," the Commissioner told the agent. "And I'll also assign to you the patrolman who might remember him. As far as I'm concerned, the whole New York police force is at your disposal. Good luck!"

With such help, the Secret Service found him after

a week-long search of rooming houses and apartment buildings. He was a sullen, shambling elevator operator, sixty years old, a mental case who should have been in a hospital long before.

He has been in an institution now for more than two years. The other day the Secret Service got this report on him:

"His mental condition appears unimproved."

15
"I Will Kill You!"

The Secret Service puzzled long over a letter from
St. Louis with a direct and deadly threat in it.

Here is the letter, addressed to "Mister Eisenhower":

> Dear mister Eisenhower
> I am mad at you and if you get elected
> another term I will kill you. every one
> knows you are a jerk and a bum.
> and another thing you better resign by
> next week or I will kill you. I am going
> to washington D. C. and then I am going
> to the white house and we will kill you.
> we would not like any trouble so you
> ~~will~~ better resign by next week
>
>   Signed by
>   Billy, M.

Was it a real threat? The Secret Service couldn't be sure. Agents searched and re-searched their indexed file, and found no other letters with the expression "you are a jerk and a bum," and no others that had told the President "you better resign."

The handwriting was childish, and the name "Billy" suggested that a child could have written the letter. But those few words, "I will kill you," were anything but childish.

Besides, many of the mentally ill have immature writing. And if the Secret Service is to do its duty to protect the President, it must take every direct threat seriously.

Only one clue amounted to anything. The letter was written on ruled paper, apparently torn from a pad, with this printed heading:

CUDAHY

OLD DUTCH CLEANSER DEPT.

SALESMEN CORRESPONDENCE

Long ago, the Cudahy company had given such pads to its salesmen who sold Old Dutch Cleanser. But it had not printed or issued the pads for several years.

The only thing for the Secret Service to do, as a start, was to interview all the men who had been salesmen of Old Dutch in the St. Louis area. The very thought of so much work made the agents weary before they began. But they had to do it because the most urgent of all their duties is investigating threats to the President.

Day after day they wore out shoe leather on the St. Louis streets. Day after day they rang doorbells and interviewed former salesmen. After nine days of tiresome interviews an agent finally found one man who remembered the printed pads.

"Yes," he said, "I did give one of these pads to

my boy. But his name is Jimmy, not Billy—and anyway, our boy would never have written such a thing."

The Secret Service man hurried to Jimmy's school. He found that Jimmy had given some of the paper to a friend in the fourth grade named Billy. The principal of the school sternly summoned Billy to his office.

Billy looked like a happy, normal boy with brown hair and sparkling blue eyes. He was wearing a yellow and white plaid shirt and a pair of blue jeans, like millions of boys in thousands of other American fourth grades.

"Billy, did you write this letter?" the principal asked.

"Yes, I wrote it. I don't know why. I wrote it in the classroom while our teacher was busy with other kids."

Billy was still smiling when the principal turned to the Secret Service officer.

"Now," said the principal, "you tell this boy who you are."

"Billy," said the agent, "I'm an agent of the United States Secret Service. What you have done is not a joke; it is a crime. A grown person can be sent to prison for five years for writing a letter like that."

The smile left Billy's face. He turned pale and looked scared.

Billy did not go to jail or to a reformatory. He and two school friends who helped him to write, stamp and mail the letter were good students. They had never been in trouble, at home or in the classroom.

But the United States Attorney in St. Louis warned the parents that if the boys wrote or mailed a similar letter in the future, "judicial action" would follow —meaning an arrest, a trial in a juvenile court, and maybe a reformatory sentence.

What Billy's parents did is a private matter between them and their son. They assured the Government that it wouldn't happen again.

Billy had cost the Government perhaps a hundred hours of time and a good many dollars in the search to find him. His name will stay on the Secret Service records, so that if he writes threats again when he grows up he can be caught with less trouble.

A letter something like Billy's, but not so hard to trace, came not long ago with an Atlanta postmark.

It was oddly different from any other letter in the Secret Service files.

It said that if the President didn't agree to form a new state in the Union, he would find himself facing a twenty-two caliber Winchester rifle. The letter was signed "King Harry I of Harrisonia."

Looking for persons named Harrison in Atlanta, and tracing the letter paper to the shop where it was bought, the Secret Service found the writer with comparatively little trouble. He turned out to be the intelligent twelve-year-old son of a scientist.

Why had the boy written it?

He had sent a box top back to a breakfast-cereal company, and in return had received a certificate making him the owner of one square inch of land in Alaska. Harry's friends also sent the box tops, and also became landowners. All the boys decided to band together and form their own state on their Alaskan land.

Harry did not realize the seriousness of what he had done. When the Secret Service explained it to him, he threw up both hands and said:

"I surrender! I am now a citizen again."

Like Billy, like others of his age who have written such letters, the Harrison boy will have his life somewhat clouded because he had let his over-active imagination run away with him. His name, too, will stay in the files.

The Secret Service has no sense of humor, and should have none, where threats to the President are concerned.

16
Visitors at the Gate

Several times every week some hopeful stranger comes to the northwest gate of the White House and demands to see the President—at once.

The uniformed White House policeman on duty has a list of the few important people who have an appointment with the President on that day.

"Have you an appointment?" he asks politely.

"No," the stranger usually answers, "but I must see him right away."

This is the signal for the Secret Service to swing into action. The policeman escorts his visitor into the little white guard building just inside the iron fence that surrounds the White House grounds.

"Would you wait just a few minutes, please? I'll send for a special assistant." The policeman then calls—for a Secret Service agent.

Not long ago an agent, asked to come quickly, found a powerfully built man waiting for him.

"The President's a very busy man," the agent said. "His appointments are all made in advance. Would you mind writing your name on this piece of paper?"

When the paper was signed, the agent passed it, without saying a word, to the policeman. The policeman went into the next room to telephone.

"Now," the agent went on, "perhaps you'd tell me what you want to see the President about."

"It's very important," the visitor said. "You see, the President and I came here together, long ago, from Mars."

"From Mars, did you say?"

"Yes, from Mars. He knows me very well. But we've been here a long time now, and it's time we started back where we came from. It will be easy. I just want to give him a couple of razor blades to slash his wrists—and I'll do the same to mine."

Before the interview was over, the agent found three razor blades strapped to his visitor's ankles. The talk was polite from start to finish. Bit by bit, the agent drew out the stranger's story. But in the end, a Secret Service car took the "Man from Mars" away for observation in a mental hospital.

Most of such visitors turn out to be mentally ill. Nowadays, few healthy Americans would expect to be ushered into the President's office without notice, or without official business to transact.

In the early days of the Republic, Presidents kept their doors open to callers, at least during certain hours. Until the time of President Hoover in 1929, you could shake hands with the President on public reception days simply by going to your Congressman and getting a ticket to the White House.

Mr. Hoover ordered the practice stopped when he found a line of a thousand men, women and children waiting for him one morning. Any President today would find it impossible to do his work if he had to spend so much time handshaking.

Besides, the Secret Service wouldn't permit it.

Among these lines of handshakers might be some mentally disturbed visitor who had slipped into the White House to harm the President. At the White House gate, at least, the Secret Service can ward off such dangers.

It is odd that more unannounced strangers come to the gate in weeks when the moon is full than at any other time. The ancient Romans used to think there was a connection between the full moon and mental illness. From this we get the old-fashioned and outworn word "lunatic" for an insane person—from the Latin word "luna" meaning "moon."

Present-day doctors know that the moon has nothing to do with it. Yet Secret Service records show that at the White House gate, at least, the full moon seems to bring out people suffering from the "Presidential complex."

Their reasons usually differ, but their object is almost always the same—to get close to the President, and in a hurry.

White House policemen have not forgotten an elderly couple who came to the gate several years ago. The husband might have been a retired school principal; the wife was a sweet-looking, white-haired type like the grandmothers in magazine advertisements. They, too, wanted to see the President urgently.

When the husband learned that it was impossible, he jumped up from the table, ran out to the street, dashed around the outside of the fence to a side street, and climbed the fence like an athlete. Police had a struggle to subdue him on the White House lawn, just outside the entrance to the Executive Office where the President works.

The wife waited quietly and did not seem concerned. The Secret Service agent asked her:

"Don't you think your husband is acting peculiarly to do a thing like that?"

She drew herself up firmly, proudly, and answered:

"I don't see that it's peculiar at all."

It turned out that the wife had a long history of mental illness; the husband had none. But by one of the rarest and saddest freaks of mental illness, both were suffering from what is called in the mental hospitals "folie à deux"—a French term meaning double insanity. Over the years the husband had adopted the wife's delusions as his own and had come to believe them just as firmly as she did.

The Secret Service liked this couple and was sorry for them and wished that treatment in a mental hospital might cure them. The agents and police almost always feel sorry for these visitors—but can take no chances with them.

As soon as the interviewing agent has taken a visitor's name, a policeman telephones it to the nearby office of the Protective Research section, in Room 98. There the file of fifteen thousand threats is searched to see whether anyone of the same name has written a dangerous letter.

The public seldom hears of the pathetic dramas that take place in the little building inside the White House fence. Almost never is there a scuffle, a shot, a disturbance that might attract public attention.

The Secret Service tries to regard these people as ill, not criminal; to protect their rights as citizens; and to help them get the mental treatment they need. For this reason, it never takes them away in a police patrol wagon; it always uses a car that looks no different from any other. It's all a part of the alert and patient work of the Secret Service in doing its sworn duty—to protect the President from harm.

17
Close Calls

For those who like to read and study history, a pleasant game is to guess what would have happened if battles, elections or other great events had turned out differently.

What would have happened, for example, if Lincoln had not been killed on April 14, 1865? What if an assassin's bullet had not put Theodore Roosevelt in the White House in 1901, with ideas so different from those of the murdered McKinley?

Nobody can ever win this game, since nobody can be sure of the answers. Yet the pastime goes on endlessly, and nowhere more often than among those who work for the Secret Service. The record of protecting Presidents is full of narrow escapes, of moments that came close to changing the course of history.

One such moment, the first of its kind in the United States, came in 1835, when there was no Secret Service, when Andrew Jackson lived in the White House. Jackson decided to go to the Capitol building for the funeral of a Congressman from South Carolina. The President had been ill; he looked gray, thin, feeble. An English visitor who saw him there wrote that he looked "scarcely able to go through this ceremonial."

As Jackson, leaning on a cane, walked slowly out of the Capitol to the top of the front steps, a black-bearded man darted out from behind one of the towering Corinthian columns. A crack like the sound of a cap pistol echoed against the stone walls as loudly as a rifle shot.

Members of the Cabinet and Congress, below the President on the steps, scattered as they heard the shot. Some of them lunged toward the man who had fired.

The President himself was not too weak to lift his cane and charge toward the bearded man. For a few tense seconds "Old Hickory" was again the dashing young general at the Battle of New Orleans.

The assassin dropped his shining pistol, whipped out another, and fired again. This time his weapon almost touched the President's chest. Again a crack split the air, as if a boy had fired a cap pistol or a small firecracker. But the President was still on his feet.

Livid with anger, Jackson wanted to thrash the man with his cane.

"Let me alone!" the old President snapped at those who were trying to hold him back. But by this time a Navy officer had leaped toward the assassin and pulled him to the ground. Two Congressmen jumped on top of the struggling men, to make sure that the attacker would not get away.

Why hadn't Jackson been killed? The percussion caps of both pistols had gone off, but by two incredible strokes of luck in quick succession they had failed to light the gunpowder and pierce the President with bullet wounds. A pistol expert said afterward that two such misfires could happen only once in 125,000 times.

The assassin was an Englishman named Richard Lawrence. He had threatened the President before and once had visited Jackson in his office to ask for a thousand dollars. He was found to be insane and spent the rest of his life in mental institutions.

In our own century, when the Secret Service has guarded nine Presidents, men like Lawrence have been watched in advance. Yet Presidents have had several narrow escapes.

One of them was Theodore Roosevelt, who thought no bullet could ever touch him. It was Roosevelt's habit to spend most evenings in his study and receive important visitors, by appointment, between nine and ten o'clock.

One evening a man drove up to the door in full evening dress—white tie and tails, high collar, opera cloak and top hat.

"The President is expecting me," he said grandly to the usher at the entrance. He gave the usher his name and a visiting card.

He left his cloak and hat and was asked to wait a few minutes in the Red Room. An usher opened the door of the President's study.

"Mr. President," he said, "here's a card from a gentleman who is in the Red Room. He says you are expecting him."

"I don't know of any such man," Roosevelt said impatiently. The usher started to leave.

"Wait!" the President called after him. "I'll go downstairs to see him. I do have a faint recollection of asking someone to come in this evening."

The President bounded down the stairs and shook hands with the stranger in the Red Room. The doors closed. Within a few minutes the buzzer at the Chief Usher's office rang violently.

The usher hurried toward the Red Room. He met the President walking toward him and saying, very calmly:

"Take this crank out of here!"

The man was hustled out and searched. In his back trousers pocket he had a powerful revolver. He had slipped past all the men, including the Secret Service agents, who should have kept him out. The Secret Service of those days had let the President down, and the usher who had let the stranger in was suspended from his job for a month without pay.

The most frightening of all such "might-have-beens" shook the nation in February, 1933, after

Franklin Roosevelt had been elected and just before he was to take the oath of office.

The President-elect had landed in Miami after a pleasure cruise along the Florida coast. He drove gaily in an open blue car to Bayfront Park, where a crowd of 8,000 had packed an open-air amphitheater to hear him.

Because Roosevelt had been crippled by polio as a younger man, he did not try to climb up to the speaker's platform. Instead, his car rolled in front of it, below the stage, and Roosevelt made his very brief speech perched high on top of the back seat of his car.

A small man with intense, dark eyes and bushy hair had been trying to find a seat and had pushed his way toward the front of the crowd. Roosevelt finished the speech and slid down onto the back seat. Instead of driving off at once, he ordered the driver to wait while he read a huge imitation telegram of welcome.

At that moment, as the crowd was leaving, the bushy-haired man jumped onto an empty seat—and fired five times.

The seat was wobbly. The man did not aim well. Instead of hitting Roosevelt, he hit the Mayor of

Chicago, Anton Cermak, who had come down from the speaker's platform to chat with the President-elect.

"I'm all right! I'm all right!" Roosevelt shouted to reassure the crowd. But the Mayor died in the hospital.

Giuseppe Zangara, the assassin, was a sick immigrant with a grudge against all government, all religion, all authority. At his trial for killing the Mayor, he admitted that he would have killed President Hoover instead of Roosevelt if he had had the chance.

Present-day doctors would have found him insane. But he was found guilty of murder and was put to death in the electric chair.

If his aim had been just a little straighter, if the seat from which he shot had been steadier, if the crowd had not blocked his aim when Roosevelt was in full view, if Roosevelt had not slid down onto the seat of the car—if any of these things had happened, American history would surely have been wrenched out of its course.

The Vice-President-elect, John N. Garner of Texas, would have gone to the White House instead of

Roosevelt. Since Garner disliked many of Roosevelt's ideas and plans, the New Deal of the 1930's might never have come to birth.

And America would have had a different leader in the Second World War which began only six years later.

The Miami shooting was the first actual attempt to kill a leader who was under Secret Service protection. Of course the Secret Service could not have watched everyone in the crowd of 8,000; it never can. On such occasions the guards can only keep the President as far as possible from anyone who might try to harm him.

But Secret Service men are frank to admit that they broke one of their foremost rules at Miami. They should not have let Roosevelt stop to read the telegram after his speech. Nowadays, when the President rides in a procession, the Secret Service insists on keeping his car moving; and nobody, however important, is allowed to stop it for any reason until it reaches its scheduled stopping place.

In wartime it was also a Secret Service job to protect the many foreign kings, queens and prime ministers who came to visit Roosevelt. Today this duty has shifted to a special security unit in the State Department—and the Secret Service is glad of it.

When Winston Churchill was about to fly home from Baltimore in 1942, after a visit to Washington, a Secret Service agent noticed a plain-clothes guard standing near the entrance to the plane. The guard was muttering and talking to himself.

"I'm going to kill that man!" the guard said. He was an American whom the British airplane company had hired for temporary duty.

The Secret Service man grappled with him and grabbed a pistol from his pocket. Of course he was mentally ill and had to go to an institution.

As Churchill walked to his plane, the agent in charge of the White House Secret Service men called out cheerily to him:

"Everything's fine, Sir!"

The Prime Minister never knew about his close call until long after he had returned to London.

This, too, was one of those "might-have-beens" that still make Secret Service men shiver when they think of them. You never will hear a Secret Service agent say that an assassination "can never happen." Sometimes it does.

18
The Battle of Blair House

The Secret Service will never forget the first of November, 1950.

Winter was coming soon, but Washington basked in an Indian Summer sun. The thermometer hit 84 degrees soon after lunchtime. Washingtonians who had to be indoors threw their windows open. Those on the streets sauntered along with a relaxed and easy air.

The President, Harry Truman, felt relaxed too. He had worked hard on the Korean War and other problems, but he decided to go home from his White House office for lunch and a nap.

"Home" in that year was not the White House. The inside of the old mansion was being torn out for a much-needed rebuilding job. The President and his family had to live at Blair House, across Pennsylvania Avenue and half a block west of the White House gate. Today it is known as the "President's Guest House."

On November 1st the Secret Service drove him, as usual, to the back entrance of Blair House, where crowds could not get too close to him. The windows and front door of the house were open except for screens. After lunch the President walked upstairs to his bedroom. He took off his outer clothes and stretched out on his bed in his underwear.

Through the screens he could hear the whir of traffic, the rattle of passing trolley cars, and even the footsteps of people walking along the sidewalk under his window. Still, he dozed within a couple of minutes. He had a way of being able to forget his troubles.

The President liked the simplicity of Blair House.

As a piece of early American architecture, it is a gem. It is really two gracious houses combined into one. The light yellow houses, one of stucco and one of brick, are almost 150 years old; in one of them Lincoln's Postmaster General, Montgomery Blair, offered Robert E. Lee the command of the Union army at the start of the Civil War.

But as a place to protect the President, the Secret Service has always detested it. Instead of having a high fence and a wide lawn in front of it, as the White House has, Blair House is built out almost to the sidewalk.

In front of the right-hand half of the combined house, as you look at it from the street, is an iron picket fence about four feet high. In front of the left-hand half there is only a tiny hedge, small enough for a child to jump over. At each end of the house, right and left, the Secret Service had built a small white booth for its guards, a few feet back from the sidewalk.

At 2:20 on the afternoon of November 1st, White House Policeman Donald T. Birdzell was patrolling the sidewalk between the booths, just in front of the steps leading to the President's front door. He heard a "click" just behind him, like the sound of a trigger that had failed to shoot. He swung around and saw a little man in a neat blue suit holding a pistol and aiming straight at him. The man pulled the trigger again, and this time hit Birdzell in his right leg.

Knowing that you have to keep moving when someone is shooting at you, Birdzell limped into the middle of the street. He dropped to one knee, whipped around and fired at the attacker.

At the same instant two guards in the booth on the right fired too. Their bullets bounced off the iron pickets of the outer fence. The attacker ran up the first two steps leading to the President's house, fired back, and then ducked low to reload.

Bullets whizzed past him. One hit him in the chest and flattened him. If he had charged up the steps to the front door, as he had planned, it would have been the end of him. Another Secret Service man in the front hallway had just set up a submachine gun, ready to blaze away at anyone who tried to enter the front screen door.

Police and Secret Service agents dashed to the scene as they heard the bullets. The traffic policeman at the next street corner rushed to a drugstore and put in an alarm. Soon the sirens were shrieking, and all that part of Washington knew that something serious was happening near the White House.

The President, hearing the shots and the sirens, jumped off his bed and ran to the upstairs window. Police on the street shouted frantically at him:

"Get back! Get back!"

Nobody knew how many other assassins might be milling around in the crowd outside the window.

Meanwhile, bullets had been flying at the left end of the house too. A second attacker had walked along the sidewalk from the opposite direction just as the first was getting ready to fire. First he looked into the open window of the booth at the left of the house, where White House Policeman Leslie Coffelt was sitting.

The attacker sprang like a cat to the open door of the booth and fired three shots, holding his gun against his chest with both hands. Whirling around, he aimed at White House Policeman Joseph H. Downs at the opposite end of the house and shot him three times. Then he jumped the little hedge and fired at Birdzell, still kneeling in the middle of Pennsylvania Avenue.

As the man stood there firing, Policeman Coffelt took aim and shot him. He crumpled over, a bullet in his brain. Then Coffelt fainted and toppled to the ground. The three shots through the door had wounded him fatally. Less than four hours later he died in the hospital.

When the gunfire stopped, the first attacker lay sprawled on the sidewalk, wounded but breathing, in front of the President's entrance. The second was dead. Among the White House guards, Coffelt was dying and Downs and Birdzell were seriously hurt.

Who were these desperate men who had tried to shoot their way into the President's house? Secret Service men, bending over the bodies, found that the first of them, the wounded man, was Oscar Collazo; the second, the dead man, was Griselio Torresola. Both were members of the small but violent nationalist group in Puerto Rico.

That overcrowded island in the Caribbean Sea, half as big as New Jersey, is a part of the United States. Although it is not a state, its people now elect their own governor and Congress, and have their own constitution. They have voted to keep their present status as a self-governing "Commonwealth" of the United States. As American citizens, they know they can sell their sugar crop to the mainland without tariffs, and they can move around the United States as freely as any other Americans. They could not do either of these things if they were a separate country.

But the Nationalist group, with no more than 500 members in Puerto Rico and even fewer in the United States, goes on plotting, and sometimes shooting, for full independence. Collazo, who survived his wounds, was one of its leading agents in New York. He was a fanatic who was ready to die for a hopeless cause. He thought that if he killed the President he would attract the world's attention and sympathy to the Nationalists. Torresola, the gunman who was killed, was another member of the group.

Clearly Collazo was different from the other assassins who killed three Presidents and tried to kill two more. His mind was on fire with what he honestly believed to be the wrongs of his people. A jury found him guilty of Coffelt's murder, and the judge sentenced him to die in the electric chair. But President Truman, the man he tried to kill, changed the sentence to one of imprisonment for life.

The Battle of Blair House rang alarm bells in the minds of Secret Service men, and goes on ringing to this day. It brought the Secret Service face to face again with the problem of political murder, of assassination that is not just the impulse of one man's disordered mind. The Nazis and Fascists of the Second World War presented a similar problem; the Communists do so today.

What worries the Secret Service is not that the leaders of such movements may try to kill the President themselves. The greater danger is that a party of violence may work on the mind of some new or unimportant member, and may lead him to do what the Puerto Ricans tried to do at Blair House.

For this reason the Secret Service does not confine its watch to the pitiful mental patients who write threatening letters or wander to the White House gate. In protecting the President, it also looks quietly into the background of anyone who may come near him. The Battle of Blair House was a warning to be on guard against political fanatics.

If Secret Service men need any further warning,

they can get it any day they walk past Blair House. For on the little picket fence is a tablet, dedicated by President Truman in 1952:

IN HONOR OF
LESLIE COFFELT
WHITE HOUSE GUARD
WHO GAVE HIS LIFE IN DEFENSE OF
THE PRESIDENT OF THE UNITED STATES
HERE AT BLAIR HOUSE, NOVEMBER 1, 1950

"FOR LOYALTY, BRAVERY AND HEROISM
BEYOND THE CALL OF DUTY"

19
The Secret Service Today

In early April every President enjoys going to Washington's ball park for the opening of the major league season. He sits in a box along the first base line.

A band plays "Hail to the Chief!" with the usual flourish of bugles and ruffles of drums as he enters the stadium. The crowd roars an ovation to him. A singer bellows "The Star-Spangled Banner" into a loud-speaker. Photographers pop their flash bulbs in front of the box as the President throws out the first ball.

"Play ball!" The game is on and the season too.

At this moment, if you are looking at the President instead of the pitcher or batter, you can see a tall fellow in a white home-team uniform standing on the sidelines in front of the box. He could be a substitute ready for a call to the line-up.

But unlike other substitutes, he wears a fielder's glove all through the game, even when his own team is batting. He isn't a substitute at all. He is a Washington player stationed in front of the box—at the request of the Secret Service—to prevent any foul from hitting the President.

To make doubly sure, Jim Rowley, the special agent in charge of the White House Detail, sometimes wears a glove, too, as he sits next to the President or behind him. Rowley was an athlete at George Washington High School in New York before he became a Secret Service agent. If a foul ever sails into the President's box, Rowley will know how to jump and catch it.

The Secret Service thinks of everything in doing its sworn duty to protect the President from harm.

So that nobody can poison him, its agents quietly

check the names and records of the staff at every market that supplies the President with food. A Secret Service man accompanies the food packages in White House trucks, so nobody can tamper with them between the shop and the White House kitchen.

If the President goes to the theater, the records of actors, ushers and stage hands are checked in advance. One Secret Service agent sits behind the President, others stand watching the audience, and still others are on guard in the wings of the stage. If a pistol has to be used in the play, a Secret Service man holds it until the actor needs it, makes sure it is unloaded or loaded with blanks, and gets it back again the moment the shooting scene is over.

To some Presidents, all this watching and guarding is a form of tyranny. Theodore Roosevelt and Harding hated it. Hoover welcomed it. Nowadays a President accepts it as a necessary evil and admires the thoroughness of the Secret Service in doing its job.

President Truman liked to think of the simpler days of the Republic when there was no Secret Service. He sometimes wished he could go swimming in the Potomac on summer mornings, as John Quincy Adams did without bodyguards, without even a pair of bathing trunks. A woman is supposed to have stolen President Adams' clothes from the river bank.

"The old guy didn't have my Secret Service guards," Mr. Truman wrote in his diary, "or it wouldn't have happened."

Indeed it wouldn't! Secret Service men would have been lurking in the bushes and would have kept strangers from all paths to the swimming hole. Today, when a President swims in tropical waters, as Mr. Truman often did in Florida, a Secret Service man swims near him—to protect him from sharks and to be ready for any emergency.

The Secret Service tries to make all this supervision as painless as possible for the President and his family. It assigns guards who are courteous, tactful, friendly—and firm only when they have to be.

In Washington, many of their precautions are what you would expect of a good bodyguard. White House policemen are on duty all night at stairways and elevators leading to the President's bedroom. Others patrol the corridors, and still others prowl the grounds outside.

When the President walks from his bedroom to his office, in the west wing of the White House, a Secret Service man strides alongside. The crippled

Franklin Roosevelt used to go to work in a wheel chair. He enjoyed whirling along the corridors so fast that the Secret Service man had to sprint to keep up with him.

When a President travels, the protective machine has to meet its hardest tests. Many weeks in advance, White House secretaries send the Secret Service, in confidence, a schedule of the out-of-town trips planned by the President. Field offices get to work quietly and secretly to check on all those who will come close to the President during his visit.

Sometimes the President decides to make a trip without much advance notice, as General Eisenhower did just after the New England floods of 1955. On such occasions, Room 98 gets a phone call from Chief Baughman of the Secret Service.

"The President's going to fly to Hartford in three days," he may say. "What have you got on it?"

The cards from Hartford are pulled from the file, showing who has written threatening letters from the area. An advance agent flies from Washington with these records. Others from the nearest field office, at New Haven, are already at Hartford checking arrangements for the President's visit.

Every potentially dangerous person has to be interviewed. The relatives usually agree to keep him at home during the President's stay. If they do not agree, the local police assign men to watch him or to keep him out of trouble.

The advance agents note and check the names of all those who will greet the President, those who will cook and serve his food, even those who will play in the band at the civic reception. If the President is to stay at a hotel, the management often clears an entire floor for him and his group from Washington. No unknown guest may stay in the rooms directly below and above him.

Before the President leaves Washington, the advance men have checked every hotel guest and servant who will be near the President during his visit. The Chief of the Secret Service insists, too, on getting a map of the precise route through the city streets and a minute-by-minute schedule.

If the President flies, he uses his own plane. The Air Force keeps this big Constellation under guard day and night when it is not in use. If he takes a train, he travels in the Presidential car, the "Ferdinand Magellan," built in wartime for Franklin Roosevelt. Instead of standing in the open railroad yards, where some mentally unbalanced character might tamper with its wheels, this car is kept locked in a long concrete shed on a siding near the Bureau of Engraving and Printing.

From the outside, it looks like any other heavy Pullman car. But this super-car has a reinforced steel floor and bulletproof windows three inches thick, and safety gadgets too many to mention. Former agent Michael Reilly, who was in charge of the White House detail in wartime, used to say that a bomb on the track couldn't shatter it and a collision with another train wouldn't buckle it. If a trestle should collapse and hurl the train into a river, those inside the car wouldn't drown. According to Reilly, the car is as waterproof as the engine room of a battleship.

On Western or Southern railroads, where traffic is not so heavy as in the East, the Secret Service usually sends a pilot train ahead of the President's, to explode any bomb placed on the track and to test any bridge that may be weak. Before the President's train passes, railroad police examine every bridge and tunnel and place guards at all of them.

The Secret Service is just as careful about the President's travel by road. The President often rides in a bulletproof Lincoln with a Secret Service driver and an agent alongside in the front seat. A second car, filled with Secret Service men, follows and keeps up with him no matter how fast the pace. Its men have orders not to let any other car slide into line between them and the President.

Out of sight in the Secret Service car, but always ready for action, is a submachine gun.

When President Eisenhower flew to Switzerland to meet Russian, British and French leaders in 1955, some European writers thought these precautions were silly. The bulletproof car, the clearing of corridors, the supervision of food and all the rest of the Secret Service routines seemed unnecessary in the land of the simple, democratic Swiss. Who in Switzerland would ever want to harm the President?

But Chief Baughman had his reasons. When General Eisenhower was President-elect in 1953, using the Commodore Hotel in New York as his headquarters, a young man tried to crash through the wooden barrier outside the President's office. He was so violent that the New York police had to use what they call "full restraint" to arrest him.

Again, during the same period, an 18-year-old threatened to kill the President-elect when he landed in Hawaii on his way to the war front in Korea. The

Secret Service is willing to look over-cautious at times—if, in doing so, it carries out its orders from Congress.

Actually, the leaders of the Secret Service believe they now have public support in their work of fighting counterfeiters, check forgers and possible assassins. Theirs is not a pleasant job, but it has rewards not measured in medals or money.

When Chief Baughman appeared recently before the House Appropriations Committee, which must approve all spending of public funds for the coming year, an admiring Congressman said to him:

"You and your service have handled yourselves magnificently. Keep it up! The life of our President depends on it."

The Secret Service has kept its numbers small. It has not advertised itself or made itself an annoyance to anyone—except to criminals. Counterfeiting is not so extensive as it used to be. Check forging is serious only because so many Americans still let themselves be fooled by it; and as for Presidential protection, the Secret Service has made it a quiet, effective science.

All its work for the American people costs about $4,750,000 a year. This pays for the Secret Service, the White House police and the Treasury Guard Force. It is less than the cost of a single B-52 bomber. More important, the men with the star-shaped badge have been a credit to the 170 million people who employ them. Their service has been free of politics and free of scandal. And for more than fifty years, nobody has accused them seriously of failing to respect the rights of free American citizens.

Someday the President of the United States may come to your town. The bands will play "Hail to the Chief!" as he appears. The thousands on the streets will cheer him as he rides by.

Four alert-looking young men will be walking alongside his car, and others will follow in a car behind. They will not be listening to the cheers or watching the President. They will be looking intently at the crowd on the curbs and in the buildings beyond.

If the American public knew more about these men, perhaps some of the cheers would go to them too.

20
If You Want to Know More
About the Secret Service

Now that this book has introduced you to the Secret Service, one way to get better acquainted with it is to come to Washington if you can. For Washington has been the headquarters of the Secret Service since 1865 and the scene of some of the most dramatic events in Secret Service history.

Anyone who is interested in the war against counterfeiters, and in the protection of Presidents, should put two "musts" on the list of places to see in Washington.

The first is the exhibit room on the first floor of the Treasury Building, just to the right of the great Ionic columns as you enter from East Executive Avenue. Here you will see the actual plates, presses and tools used by notorious counterfeiters who went to prison. On the walls and in showcases are examples of some of the most deceptive counterfeit money ever made.

Here, too, you will see the revolver Czolgosz used to shoot McKinley, the official certificate of his execution at Auburn Prison, and other exhibits dealing with attempts to murder Presidents. The Treasury exhibit room is open to the public Mondays through Fridays from 9:30 A.M. to 1 P.M.

The second "must" on your list should be a visit to the Bureau of Engraving and Printing, where all United States paper money, savings bonds and postage stamps are made.

Guides will escort you through rooms where millions of dollars are being printed in huge sheets, then counted, cut and bundled for distribution before your eyes. They will show you, too, millions of postage stamps being printed, gummed and packaged.

Visitors are welcome in these sections of the Bureau Mondays throught Fridays, from 8 to 11 A.M. and from 12:30 to 2:00 P.M. Exhibits in the lobby will show you specimens of every kind of paper money and postage stamp issued by the United States in the last hundred years—even to that rarity, a $100,-000 bill, which is used only in government or bank dealings. The engraving and numbering of paper money takes place in rooms which are closed to the public.

Ford's Theater building, where Lincoln was shot, still stands on Tenth Street, Northwest. Across the street, unaltered through the years and open to the public, is the house where Lincoln died. The theater itself no longer exists, but on the first floor of the theater building is a Lincoln museum with many letters, pictures and relics of the Emancipator.

The railroad station where Guiteau shot Garfield was torn down many years ago. The National Gallery of Art now stands on the site.

Blair House, where the Puerto Ricans tried to shoot President Truman, is a landmark on Pennsylvania Avenue, across the street and half a block west of the White House. Since Blair House is the Government's home for distinguished foreign visitors, it is not open to the public. But you can walk past it and photograph it, and see in your mind's eye the gun battle that blazed on the sidewalk and street only a few years ago.

Just inside the White House gate nearest to Blair House, you can see the little white building where visitors ask for the President. The White House itself is open to visitors from 10 A.M. until noon, Tuesdays through Saturdays. Uniformed men of the White House police, a unit of the Secret Service, will watch you carefully as you file through the reception rooms and the state dining room. The President's office and living quarters are not, of course, open to the public.

If you should like to read more about the fight against counterfeiters, by far the best book on the subject is *Counterfeiting: Crime Against the People* by Lawrence Dwight Smith (1944). This book is so careful and thorough that it is required reading in the Secret Service training school. In it you will find a detailed history of money and counterfeiting, a description of how paper money and coins are made and imitated, and a few dramatic stories of counterfeiters who went to jail.

You can find other stories of counterfeiters in *Our United States Secret Service* by Irving Crump (1942) and *Men Against Crime* by J. J. Floherty (1946). The exploits of Pinkerton's men in the Civil War are best described in the newly-republished *Photographic History of the Civil War*, in the volume entitled *Soldier Life and Secret Service*. The first volume of Carl Sandburg's magnificent *Abraham Lincoln: the War Years* (1939) tells of Lincoln's secret trip through Baltimore to escape assassination. The last volume re-creates, in almost minute-to-minute detail, the night of his murder in Ford's Theater.

On Presidential protection, the outstanding book is *The Assassins* by Robert J. Donovan (1952). As the title suggests, the book deals chiefly with the background, character and motives of each of the strange men who killed or tried to kill a President. It also tells, vividly and honestly, what happened at each assassination, and how the Secret Service protects the President today.

Two chiefs of the White House Detail of the Secret Service have written books about their experiences. Both are packed with good stories about Presidents and their families. The livelier of the two books, *Reilly of the White House* by William J. Slocum and Michael F. Reilly (1947), recalls many of the nerve-racking moments the Secret Service had while guarding Franklin D. Roosevelt at home and on his wartime trips abroad.

The other, *Starling of the White House* by Thomas Sugrue and Colonel Edmund W. Starling (1946) is the story of the charming Kentucky gentleman who was part bodyguard, part companion, of five Presidents from Woodrow Wilson to Franklin Roosevelt.

The best short accounts of the Secret Service are two clearly written, well-produced government pamphlets: "Know Your Money" (1955) and "The United States Secret Service: What It Is, What It Does" (1955). You can buy or order these for 20 cents each from the Superintendent of Documents, U. S. Government Printing Office. Washington 25, D. C. Many of the pictures in this Landmark book were reprinted from these pamphlets by permission of Chief Baughman and the Secret Service.

Index

The Legend of Zelda Breath of The Wild Nintendo Switch Game Guide Unofficial

Copyright 2017 by The Yuw
Third Edition, License Notes

Copyright Info:

Legal Info:

Presented by HiddenStuffEntertainment.com

Table of Contents

Preface

We want to take a moment to say thank you for purchasing our strategy guide online. HiddenStuff Entertainment remains one of the top app and eBook publishers online. It is our commitment to bring you the latest support and strategies for today's most popular games.

We sincerely hope that you find this guide useful and beneficial in your quest for digital immortality. We want to provide gamers with knowledge and build their skills to perform at the highest levels within their games. This in turn contributes to a positive and more enjoyable experience. After all, it is our belief that things in life are to be enjoyed as much as they possibly can be.

If you game on a regular basis and are involved in some of the top titles online, we wanted to extend a special offer to gain access to free resources provided exclusively by us.

As an added bonus to your purchase please follow the "CLICK HERE" link below to sign-up for our free eBooks and guides program. Here you will receive free guides and resources for today's most popular games, mobile apps, and devices! Sing-up for free below. It's our way of saying thanks for being a valued customer!

CLICK HERE TO SIGN-UP FOR FREE

How to Install the Game for Wii U

1) Start your Wii U System.

2) Sign-in to your account. Please note, if you do not have an account you can use the "Create Account" button below the sign-in page as pictured below.

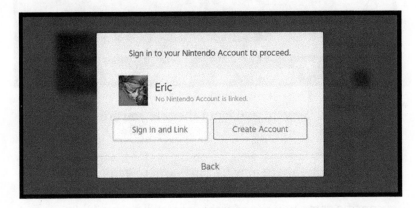

Sign in to your Nintendo Account to proceed.

Eric
No Nintendo Account is linked.

| Sign In and Link | Create Account |

Back

3) Once signed in, go to the Nintendo Store on your home screen or visit:
http://www.nintendo.com/wiiu/eshop/virtual-console/

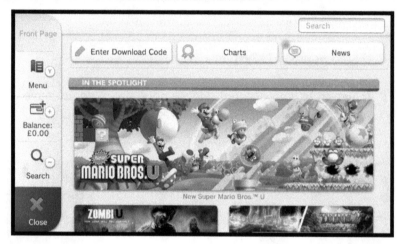

4) Click on "Search" and input the title you are searching for.

*Please note- there may be times where games and or content are unavailable. We cannot guarantee that the specific game you are searching for will be available.

5) Once you locate the title you are searching for, click the "Download" button as shown in the screenshot below.

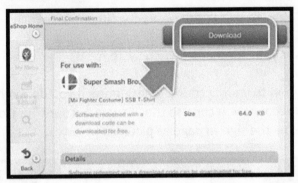

6) Once your game has downloaded it will be ready to play by visiting the home screen.

How to Install the Game for Nintendo Switch

1) Start your Nintendo Switch System.

2) Sign-in to your account. Please note, if you do not have an account you can use the "Create Account" button below the sign-in page as pictured below.

3) Once signed in, go to the Nintendo Store on your home screen or visit:
http://www.nintendo.com/switch/online-service/

4) Click on "Search" and input the title you are searching for.

*Please note- there may be times where games and or content are unavailable. We cannot guarantee that the specific game you are searching for will be available.

5) Once you locate the title you are searching for, click the "Download" button as shown in the screenshot below.

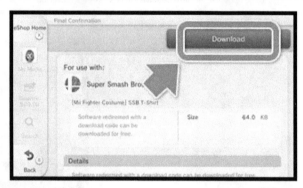

6) Once your game has downloaded it will be ready to play by visiting the home screen.

Introduction

"The Legend of Zelda: Breath of the Wild's" launch comes about on "the Great Plateau", that is packed with secrets, concealed goods as well as treasure. We will document your canonical ventures, elevating the tower, locating and conquering the shrines, acquiring the para-glider and much more in our walkthrough. In this tutorial, we will exhibit "the Great Plateau's" tricks, of which, the majority incorporates excellent early game weaponry, rookie tips, and a complete game walkthrough.

"The great plateau" is almost the entire game

You start "The Legend of Zelda: Breath of the Wild" on the "Great Plateau", the geological-skyscraper overlooking the huge Empire of Hyrule. There are many mountains to climb up, jungles to plunder, wildlife to fight and dungeons to conquer. Within the early hours of the game, you will be caught up here, within a microcosm of the entire Zelda world.

Though you cannot yet examine larger world, almost everything you do (and plenty of the things you might not even realize that can be done) acts like a prologue to the time ahead.

For example, the way to create your path towards Hyrule properly and effectively. We take care of this in our "Great

Plateau" walkthrough. But do not imagine "Breath of the Wild's" as a game to finish quickly and haphazardly. The time period you invest at this point is extremely important. The abilities and patterns you find while you navigate "the Great Plateau" are going to prove to be just as relevant as the time afterwards when you are on a different side of the world. "Breath of the Wild" does not inform you of this however, you will find out soon enough. In the subsequent sections, we will present the implicit facts and provide some recommendations about how exactly you ought to consider playing this fantastically amazing game.

Discover, fight and acquire

Recently, Designers started giving gamers a helping hand. Die a couple of times in Mario game, for instance, and game presents you a power up which makes conquering the level simpler. It is philosophy aimed at accessibility as well as assisting everybody succeeds without disgrace.

"The Legend of Zelda: Breath of the Wild" seems that it was developed with a different perspective in mind.

To Zelda followers, "Breath of the Wild" may feel familiar as well as accessible, nevertheless designers are less bothered with holding your hand. Rather than that, they're with persuading you to try things out and discover. The game seldom notifies you just where to look or how to proceed in detail. Rather, it likes to wink or nudge content to allow you

to fill up the spaces. In the game, you can do anything you would like to and you will find that there are plenty of hidden surprises along the way.

Put in a different way, "Breath of the Wild" abounds with hints and clues, not really directions. Plus a surprising number of the strategies you will work with during the entire game, appear in initial hours, even though you do not realize it.

On "the Great Plateau", you are supposed to discover, fight as well as collect. Sixty or so hours later, you are also meant to explore attack and accumulate. To carry out what you have previously done, just simply on a much grander level. Do not be in a rush to leave. There is a great deal to learn and lots of time to try out.

How can you realize what to discover, just who to fight and exactly to collect? Generally by employing the logic which you acquired during your early hours discovering the game. All of it makes sense. Just keep in mind simple stuff like precisely how to survive against cold weather, exactly how opponents have all the tools you require, and that communicating is actually a subtle yet crucial element of exploration.

Be social and also friendly

Within the game you are not directed on how to "socialize" and interact with others. The simplest way to determine what is next is to be chatty. Start conversations and socialize. Communicate with everyone in the game. Several conversations may end in just one minute, serving mainly as a way to really make the environment feel lively and more real. Some other discussions will provide you with hints about what to accomplish and how you might go about doing it. It is not easy to tell who is helpful and who is likely to complain about weather, so becoming chatty is a good move to make.

Worst scenario, you can slam buttons and just forward through discussions that go nowhere. Whereas, the best scenario, you run into the very handy reoccurring people in "Breath of the Wild" who provide missing explorers direction. A beginning game instance shows exactly this. Once you finish the 1st major missions, you will leave a building without any idea of what to do next.

Just down a few steps away from exit, though, you will see a non-descript personality. You are free to speak with or even overlook him. If you do not speak with him, perhaps you can simply surf around and also wish you come across the plot. In the case that you speak to him, you will discover that he is actually created to provide you with clues about a quest and not simply here but during the entire game.

This is the way "Breath of the Wild" works. It would like you to act as a detective, instead of telling you what to do. However, in case you do need to know, it will also provide you with this resource.

Additional Benefits & Side Quests

Chatting to NPCs as well, opens side quests and it is simple to recognize the specific characters who extend your game and provide additional opportunities.

When you find a word-bubble having a red exclamation in its top left corner, that is "Breath of the Wild" indicating that there is a mission available from this specific character. The small guy in the image has a full backstory regarding his grandpa and also a fascination with the "weapons of Hyrule". Such as in most games, side missions are an option. You do not have to discover them, and in some cases if you carry them out, you do not have to complete them. But they are packed with incentives and rewards that vary in size. Nintendo has peppered the" Hyrule's landscape" with these.

Speak to people. Understand the things they want. Do what appears fun and abandon what remains.

Fighting Enemies

When you are not shooting the breeze with other characters, you will be doing lots of battling. Combat in "Breath of the Wild" is simple, but there're several things worth talking about.

1st, fighting enemies is difficult. It will not take you long to bump into an adversary who can easily clobber all of your hearts out using 1 swing of his "spiked club". Opponents can and will overpower you, so do not imagine you are stronger than you actually are.

If you get engaged in melee fight, it is usually a smart idea to concentrate on enemies using the ZL button, however it is not at all times necessary. Even when you are locked on, camera angles can be misleading. When this occurs, launch ZL, point the right thumbstick on the foe you intend to hit, and following this swing away. "Breath of the Wild" is likely to link your weapon with the opponent, even if you are not zeroed in.

When you are utilizing ranged weaponry such as the bow and arrows, headshots matter. However remember that they are not always conclusive to eliminating the enemy in one-hit. The bigger number of damage that your bow has, the greater destruction it will cause. Some bows will not have a superior base harm to kill your foe in a single strike to the head. Additionally, many opponents have got more health

compared to you but you can eradicate using a single arrow, so do not depend on headshots just for quick kills.

In addition, provide accurate targeting using the Joy-Con movement controls provided. It might take a little bit of getting familiar with however, Nintendo fine-tuned the precision so that it is perfectly feasible and a very fast method to shoot simply above a head as well as lock-in your arrow's arch all the way to its goal.

Advanced Fighting

A number of superior combat strategies call for precise timing. A few repel assaults. Others enable you to release a flurry of continuous counterattacks. All of them look great, plus they have a tendency to eliminate monsters, however they are also extremely hard to implement and they are not really necessary.

Here is the fact: Even if you can easily eliminate almost everything by pressing a single key, these superior methods are always accessible. They are often something that you can do to enhance your abilities, plus they are able to turn hard enemies into effortless victories, provided you have the right timing involved.

Browse the specific tutorial video from" Ta'Loh Naeg Shrine", that you can get in the borders of the "Kakariko Village". It will reveal how to perform these moves:

- "Side hop". Aim for your enemy using ZL, go right or left, push X to bounce.
- "Backflip". Aim for your enemy using ZL, go away from your opponent, push X to bounce. Push Y to follow-up side-hop as well as backflip with flurry rush, that enables you to smack away many times at your opponent as the time decreases.
- "Perfect guard". Aim for your opponent using ZL, push A to parry using your shield.

- "Charged attacks". Hold Y to construct your energy, after that let go to strike.

To reiterate, we have discovered all of these techniques in particular are very difficult to implement.

Acquiring Weapons & Inventory

We are incorporating weapons, loot as well as inventory management in this part because they are all parts of overlapping systems.

There might be a lot more weapons in "Breath of the Wild" compared to all other Zelda games put together. (And if that is untrue, it certainly seems like it). Point is, you will use plenty of weaponry and have opportunities to try many different tactics as you progress in the game.

The upshot? "Weapon proliferation" implies that you need to think much more regarding what you current have in your possession, what you require and exactly you need to use right now. In case you have got a strong weapon, do not put it to use to simply beat rocks. Each swing results in 1 less that you will take against a foe. In fact, it is a good idea to hold a heavy, unwieldy tool such as a sledgehammer for situations similar to this. Keep your spears clubs and swords for fighting meat, certainly not rocks.

Obtaining fresh weapons as well as loot is easy in concept and also execution. Opponents holding weapons will shed them once they perish or if you wallop them. When this occurs, you can grab the weapon and employ it for yourself (or perhaps thieve it away from your opponent).

This makes equipment acquisition simple, too: When you require a weapon, simply kill enemies holding weapons. Obviously, a game loaded with weapon loot drops beings up an expected query: Should you grab the tool you jarred loose? Usually, the reply is yes. There are several slots for weaponry. Load them all fully. Your tools will crack and break after use. Do not get too linked to any weapon. You will require backups as many of your weapons will break eventually.

Worst situation, maybe you do not apply everything you index. No big deal. Or perhaps it is there once your other weapons crack, and at the very least you may have one thing to work with.

You do not have to pick all the things that drop, of course, and you may make correct call without picking anything and saving it for a more desirable and useful item. Every weapon in "Breath of the Wild" contains an arrow symbol just to the right of its name, showing its attack strength, in accordance with what you are wielding right now.

- If arrow is actually green as well as directing up, then it is mightier by comparison to your current item.
- In case it is red and directed down, that means it is less effective.
- When it is gray and aiming right, this means it is the exact same grade as what you are possessing.

A fast push of the plus key, and you will see your existing arsenal. Every single weapon features a number, denoting its strength. Every time you choose a tool, it will reveal your weapon's number as well as the new weapon's number right alongside it. In case you discover anything good, shed your worst tool and grab the fresh and more powerful loot.

That is the almost all the stock management you will do in "Breath of the Wild": looking at figures against other figures and trading lowest denominator items for higher ones. You will find loads of weaponry and plenty of weapon varieties in the game. Test, determine what you prefer to employ and pile up those specific types, whether they are one handed weapons such as swords as well as clubs or even two handed tools such as halberds and spears. Construct your own toolbox.

Learning How to Cook

"Breath of the Wild" does not walk out its way to describe its cooking process. That is strange, provided how essential it truly is.

You may stroll upon the Old Person within your first hour or so, and he might inform you a little something opaque related to cooking. Or perhaps you could overlook this connection altogether and play for a long time prior to working it out by yourself. Do not do the latter. Begin preparing once and as early as you can.

There're a couple of extensive groups of things to prepare in "Breath of the Wild": food as well as elixirs. Regardless of what you are preparing, it functions the same exact way. Get to a metal bowl. Turn on fire beneath it if required. Push + to get into your inventory display, and pick upto 5 ingredients to place. Get to the bowl and when prompted, push A to prepare food. It is that easy. We'll convey more on food preparation afterwards in this tutorial.

WHAT ARE YOU INTENDING TO DO?

Perhaps some combo of "whatever the heck you want" and "find the thing that you're looking for"? It is actually entirely your decision.

We understand that seems like not an answer, but it is also a fact that the game made to provide its participants an enormous level of freedom. No 2 playthroughs would be the exact same. Our "Breath of the Wild" simply not your "Breath of the Wild". They are not intended to be. We will all start on the "Great Plateau", however where we proceed after that is basically onto our whims.

Knowing that, here are some tips, which mainly amount to exactly what we'd to continue reminding ourselves during our play time.

- It is not easy. You will perish. However that is fine since the consequence of dying is just a slight backtracking.
- It is complicated, but that is because it is an open environment game. Worst scenario, you can simply stroll off and browse through whatever vibrant thing you see. In addition there are many towers along with shrines to uncover.
- Grab items, even when you do not understand what they are for. They will probably turn out to be suddenly helpful.
- Talk to everybody. Those not having important information will not consume most of your time. Individuals with valuable details is likely to help you progress in the game.
- In case you do not understand what to accomplish, discover towers and shrines.

- When you discover something and know of its importance however, you cannot perform it at this time, place a label on your map and revisit it later. We want to tag the locations of points of interest using a leaf and also shrines we cannot accomplish through placement of a star.
- Presume that all the things are there for a purpose. When you leave a building and there is a fresh character position by the doorway who would like to speak with you, speak to them. That is "Breath of the Wild" lightly pointing you on the correct course.
- In case you would like to focus, employ fast travel. There are a large amount of distractions. That is also beauty of the game. It is possible to undertake whatever you want whenever you would like to do it. However if you happen to feel as if you intend to make advancement, fast travel to anywhere you would like to go. If you don't, it is also easy to get diverted otherwise.

The Ways to Tame a Horse

Wild Horses often gather in broad open plains, such as "Central Hyrule Field" or around "Dueling Peaks", yet can be found in number of places. In many cases the spot of wild horses tend to be linked to the strength of their pace, endurance, as well as handling, because stronger horses often stroll in more dangerous locations.

You have to be sneaky and very smart to tame a horse. It is possible to crouch to engage and also to stealth. To do so, gradually create your path toward the horse without scaring it. Get close enough to capture and after that quickly touch the "Soothe" key prior to your stamina flees in order to effectively tame it.

In case sneaking is not your thing, there is also a method to paraglide onto one however, try to be cautious. As soon as tamed, the horse might yet attempt to override your given instructions, so make sure to enroll them at a close by stable and also continue calming the horse once they begin to avoid your instructions. You may also feed apples to it in order to improve its friendliness towards you.

In case the horse you're seeking to tame turns out to be tough and you also exhausted all of your stamina, think about creating food or elixirs that boosts your stamina, or even re-supply it while in the taming procedure in order to hang on for longer intervals. It's also possible to enhance

your stamina vessel by providing four Spirit Orbs to a
Goddess Statues located in main towns and also the "Temple
of Time".

The Ways to Obtain Heart Containers

In "The Legend of Zelda: Breath of the Wild", you'll shortly see that Heart Pieces don't appear to be in Hyrule, so you will not be able to locate and boost your hearts by conventional means.

That is because there are not any. Rather, the only method you will get extra "Heart Containers" through praying to a Goddess idol in the major towns and also the "Temple of Time". These sculptures can also be found in many other villages and generally produce a glow from afar.

In return for four Spirit Orbs acquired by finishing Shrines, you can actually claim either a fresh "Heart Container" or even "Stamina Vessel".

If the opponents you are battling appear too difficult, or perhaps you have to show your inner-power, make sure to go hunting for Shrines to boost your stats.

Acquire the "Master Sword"

The "Master Sword" isn't simple to find. Absolutely no major story point can possibly steer you to it as well as actually it is possible to finish the game without even getting it.

Most of the chiefs of every race will provide you with hints to its position however in reality the "Master Sword" is concealed in the "Lost Woods", situated deep inside the "Hyrule Great Forest" located in the area to the North of "Hyrule Castle".

Moving through THE "LOST WOODS"

On the "Woodland Tower", you can view the huge forest which is obstructed on nearly all edges by water. Nevertheless, attempting to climb up or slip into the "Lost Woods" and you will be transferred by mystical laughter.

In order to enter the "Lost Woods", you have to take the route Northeast from the tower and also stick to the course right up to the vicinity. Here it becomes foggy and you also arrive at a big destroyed arch.

With regard to these following areas, deviating from route under any sort of circumstances can lead to a transportation back to last checkpoint. In such a case the "large arch". Please note that there's an illuminated torch here, plus more further away from your route.

Through 1st torch go North, to the north once again, after that West, To the west again, after that South, and lastly look West to identify 2 Torches from the distance just before a huge Ogre Tree having a chest in mouth.

From 2 torches, stuff will get even more difficult. There will be no more torches that could assist you, and when you de-track, you will be rapidly surrounded in haze and brought back towards the previous torches. In case you're fast to respond it is possible to get away from fog however it travels very quickly.

To find your path, employ a torch or any type of other combustive tool and light it on the 2 torches. Stay still and glance on the embers flying away from the top of torch. They'll be heading slightly in the course you should proceed. Continue pursuing the embers and you'll ultimately find your way to the "Korok Forest", exactly where the "Master Sword is hidden". It's a big clue for you.

GETTING THE "MASTER SWORD"

When you reach the midst of the grove, you will obtain the "Master Sword", however trying to draw it will result in abrupt vision, and also the "Great Deku Tree" will rise to talk with you.

A lot has transpired from the time the blade was carried here a century back, and only a person who has great strength can claim "the Master Sword". This involves you, despite all this time period. According to where you stand in this game, you possibly will not be worthy of this yet. In case you attempt to draw it, you'll feel that it gradually drains your hearts.

In case you don't have adequate Heart Containers, you'll never be allowed to draw it from pedestal. The 1st time you attempt, "the Great Deku Tree" will stop prior to your last heart is exhausted however afterward, you undertake it at the threat of your existence.

In reality, drawing "the Master Sword" out will need an overall 13 Heart-Containers. Having 3 hearts you start the game with, it means you will require extra ten Heart-Containers. Heart-Containers can be acquired both by exchanging in 4 Spirit-Orbs, or maybe by finishing one of many Divine-Beast Dungeons. Bearing this in mind, it will require a distinct amount of Spirit-Orbs based upon the number of dungeons you have completed. It indicates you will require up to forty Spirit-Orbs if you have not completed

any dungeons, and also as fewer as twenty four if you have carried out all, or perhaps any place in between.

Using "THE MASTER SWORD"

Even the Edge which Seals the Darkness yet needs to follow particular principles. You will find that you can utilize it everywhere, however attacking typical enemies and creatures will still wear-down the edge. At this stage it is going to seem as if the sword is busted, and may not be in condition to use for a few minutes till it regenerates.

The only situations the edge can be utilized forever not having worry about breaking is during the existence of "Ganon" or any of his incarnations, so be careful before you choose to use the sword.

Acquire the "Hylian Shield"

Link's Iconic "Hylian Shield" is concealing in this game at someplace, however isn't simple and easy to locate and in fact just about the most strong and effectively concealed things in this game.

You can find this particular shield in depths of "Hyrule Castle Dungeon". The castle by itself is a puzzle of pathways and opponents, and this specific region is easily ignored.

The easiest method to get to it is by penetrating the West part of "Hyrule Castle" and searching for entrances along side west bank which steer underground. It will ultimately send you to the "Hyrule Castle" Lockup, showcasing an extended row of cells in which a lot of strong foes roam. At the end of the hallway you will find a small passage directing to a loose rock-wall, it is possible to blow up using Remote Bombs. The area beyond is big and also filled with bones.

To be able to claim the "Hylian Shield" from this location, you first have to battle "the Stalnox", a skeletal Hinox mini-boss which is incredibly challenging and will make use of its own bones to strike you with. It can solely be harmed by targeting its eye and following it across the room to harm it prior to Stalnox get it and place it back.

Utilize Bomb-Arrows to dislodge the eye any time he is not masking it using his hand, as well as make use of strong weaponry to offer the maximum amount of damage to eye.

As soon as the Stalnox is beaten, a chest will show up having the "Hylian Shield", that offers extreme toughness along with an enormous 90 armor defense.

Buying a House

Speak to Bolson, the forman of crew, he will provide you with the opportunity to buy the house for you. It'll price at 3,000 as well as 30-bundles of timber to really make the bargain. When you purchase it, it is yours and you'll even be able to add many upgrades to it over time.

"The Great Plateau" Walkthrough

MEET UP WITH OLD MAN

You get up from a heavy sleep, and there is just one path to take. Pick up your Sheikah slate, wear clothes and go up out of the cave. Move to the right, head-down the hill and talk to the Old Man. You can grab any "Hylian shrooms" you see on the way. You can easily overlook the tree branches.

Speak to the Old Man and wear out your dialogue choices. Prior to leaving, grab the torch lying next to the wall right behind him and also the cooked apple sitting close to the fire.

ELEVATE "THE GREAT PLATEAU" TOWER

Stick to the way to the right of that Old Man and grab the woodcutter's axe that is hidden inside a tree stump. Maintain right, jump into the water and rise up to the top of the small island to grab the rustic broadsword. Be cautious here, due to the fact "Breath of the Wild" will show you the way to throw your weapon.

This time, a similar disembodied tone which woke you up from sleep will speak once again and put a sign on the map. Continue with the Sheikah-slate making use of waypoint on the map, and put this inside the terminal. It elevates "the Great Plateau Tower" (along with other towers around Hyrule).

Make your way towards the top of the tower, where you will meet the Old Man yet again. Connect using the Sheikah terminal, that will put information regarding "the Great Plateau" to the map. "The Old Man" will provide you with isolated-plateau major quest stating that he will exchange the paraglider when you conquer a shrine.

"Oman-Au Shrine" (Magnesis Trail) Guidelines

1. Get into the "Oman-Au shrine" and sync up with the terminal to have magnesis, Its power is very effective and it is to move the metal things, which is exactly the thing that you suppose to do in this particular shrine.
2. Utilize magnesis to shift the steel plates on the ground. Then bounce down and stroll from the lobby and back-up to the ground level.
3. Make use of magnesis in order to pull or even push the metallic block inside the wall.
4. Hop thru and eliminate the guardian-scout covering right behind the wall.
5. Move from the 1st to the 2nd platform, on the steel plate. Then turn-around as well as utilize magnesis to push the steel plate between the 2nd and 3rd platform.
6. Facing the gigantic doors when standing on 3rd platform, move left and utilize magnesis to draw the treasure-chest down from platform. Open it up to find the traveler's-bow, a strong bow which will offer you an advantage in the beginning of the game.
7. Utilize magnesis to be able to open the enormous doors.
8. Go up the stairways to alter and meet "Oman Au", who'll provide you with very first "spirit orb". (You will obtain one for each shrine you conquer.)

LOCATING THE 3 OTHER SHRINES

At this stage, you have completed your responsibility to old man, but he is a jerk, and changes the principles. You have to find, and conquer 3 more shrines.

Go back to the top of tower (bending is still speediest) and then press right analog stick to make use of your Sheikah slate as the makeshift telescope. You will find 3 glowing shrines; one of them in your line of sight, when you just peer through the Sheikah slate, second is at the right of that location, right up on the iced mountain, and the third is at the left (in southeast of your location). We will do the southeast one primary.

"Ja Baij Shrine" (Bomb Trial) Walkthrough

The way to Ja Baij shrine will be risky due to the presence of decayed guardians like the one enemy in the gallery. They are big, and they can not move (that is good), but they are lethal - just one hit will be deadly.

It is not really worth struggling them now, but you will need avoid them and move to the shrine. It is simple, as well. They are jammed in the ground and they are bounded by the crumbling walls. Which means you have got cover. Run between the cover, restoring your strength until you get the shrine.

1. Communicate with the terminal to find the remote bombs.
2. Set off a remote-bomb next to a couple of big cracked stones.
3. Off the passageway and then to your left, Set off another remote-bomb to demolish another pair of cracked stones.
4. Climb-up the stairway, and position a square-bomb on the far end of floating platform.
5. On far left-corner of room (just to the left of shrine), you will uncover a treasure-chest. Allow the launcher toss you onto it, here gather your amber.
6. Return to exactly where you came from and shed a round-bomb thru the tube using the large opening. It'll

fly over the room and also get to a big stack of cracked rocks. Set it off to demolish those cracked rocks cubes.

7. Jump down the room and then up the ladder. Get to the altar and also pick up your "spirit orb".

Defend Against the Cold & The "Waterfall Treasure"

The way to the approaching dungeon needs a hike as well as some ingenuity.

MAINTAINING WARMTH

In case you head into the "Great Plateau's" snowy and cold parts not having any protection, you will take damage quickly. You have to stay heated, and there is many different ways to achieve that. It is possible to:

- Cook anything using peppers then consume that for a permanent burst of prevention against cold.
- Bring a fire torch or any burning weapon.
- The former is a lot easier since you can also work with your weaponry and also shield. Simply pick any raw vegetation or meat which you have indexed, hold it, and after that decide on a hot and spicy pepper to hold, as well. Toss them in a cooking bin and consume it. You will observe that you have raised your cold defense for a particular period of time. Now you will be able to enter in the cold parts without fear of taking damage.

THE WATERFALL-TREASURE

Enter into snowy parts from west part of the map, simply turn left, and go along with the path around the water. Get

ready to fight some chuchus (keep a safe distance since they can easily freeze you)...

When you get to the damaged bridge, then use magnesis to raise the metal platform, and put it down to cover up the gap in broken bridge. Pass through the bridge, move left and always keep the lake on your right. Right behind the waterfall, you will find broadsword of the soldier, 5 arrows, 5 fire arrows, and one spiked boko bow.

The Keh-Namut Shrine

· Build the makeshift bridge with the magnesis and at the end of this bridge, move right, and travel to the mountain. You will encounter some bokoblins in your way, and a few huge snowballs. At the top of mountain, you will find the subsequent shrine.

HOW TO CONQUER THE "KEH-NAMUT SHRINE" (CRYONIS-TRIAL)

-When you arrive in Keh-Namut shrine, get help from the device to find another rune, cryonis, that enables you to change water in huge pieces of ice.

-Use cryonis to produce a massive slice of ice, and after that ascend up and through it in the next room.

-Employ cryonis to make a large piece of ice beneath sealed door.

-Use cryonis to make a ramp under the stone plank.

-Use cryonis to make a enormous slice of ice, then climb-up to get the treasure-chest where you will get a "traveler's spear".

-Enter the shrine to get your "spirit orb".

The Owa-Dam-Shrine

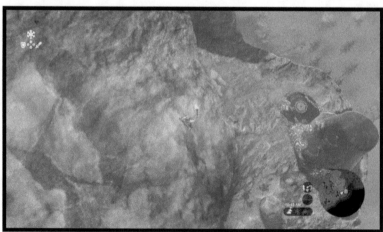

From Keh-Namut-shrine, stroll beyond fire and up to the top in the distance. Wander around that far area, take left and go on till you could see the final shrine on the cliff's edge.

CONQUER THE "OWA-DAM-SHRINE"

1. Connect to the device once you get to the "Owa-Dam-shrine" to find the next rune, statis, that allows you to decelerate plus manipulate time.
2. Employ stasis over the giant gear that is tossing the bridge ahead, then cross the bridge.
3. Carry on on the way, turn left and employ stasis to cease the moving boulders.
4. Go up to the top, open the treasure-chest as well as get a "traveler's shield".
5. Return down , take a right and grab the "iron-sledgehammer" seated next to far wall.
6. Employ stasis on immobile boulder which is obstructing your way, and wack it using the iron-sledgehammer. The momentum will establish and release the boulder in the air, allowing you to gather your "spirit orb" and leave.

When you exit the shrine, employ stasis on boulder just outside shrine's front door. You will discover a treasure-chest having the strong traveler's bow.

Mount-Hylia

Mount-Hylia is a very cold region in the "Great Plateau". The Keh-Namut-shrine rests to the west of Mount-Hylia's top and the Owa-Daim-shrine rests just out of its east side. There is a great deal to discover in the region between the both. Prior to that, ensure you are secured against the cold.

There is a simple formula to make your journey very easy: Cook 5 spicy peppers, and you will make hot sautéed peppers, which provides you 5 hearts as well as 12 mins 30 seconds of low degree cold resistance. Do not worry about title. It offers all the defense you need to make it around Mount-Hylia.

Just so you know, you do not have to cook all 5 peppers. However each pepper which you put in the recipe boosts your ability against cold. And if you are seeking hot peppers, check out the west entrance to Mount-Hylia (the particular one where you find a raft inside a lake once you walk in). There're lots around that area and there is a food preparation container inside a camp-of-bokoblins towards the eastern side of the entrance and you'll discover a lot more spicy peppers as well as be able to prepare more meals.

Additionally, if you see the Old Man while travelling, he might provide you with the warm doublet, a kind of shirt that guards you from cold. In case you do not come across him, you can buy the armor later from a vendor back in a town.

The Frigid-Pond

Inside the frigid-pond just outside the Keh-Namut-shrine, apply cryonis to make a block of ice beneath a treasure-chest. Jump in, climb up as well as open the chest for the opal.

MELTDOWN ICE FOR THE KOROK-SEED

On the ledge near the Keh-Namut-shrine, you will find a big block of ice. Whether bring a lit up torch all the way up, or you can use a few flint, and wood to set up a fire like we do

in the picture above. Either way, stay close to the snow with fire in your hand. When it starts to melt, you will soon meet a korok along with a korok seed.

ELIMINATING BOKOBLINS FOR THE TREASURE

In the way to the east of "Mount Hylia", there is actually a blue bokoblin, and a cluster of brownish bokoblins. Strike the blue bokoblin in first place, then open up the treasure chest right behind him for certain amber. Then fellow over the ledge, and combat the 3 other bokoblins by using your bow and arrow, get down, and open up the chest they were protecting for 5 arrows.

AROUND THE "OWA DAIM" SHRINE

Just out of the "Owa Daim shrine", you will get a boulder.
After finishing the shrine, and getting stasis ability, make use
of it on the boulder. Attack with a heavy weapon (sledgehammer you have got within the shrine is an ideal tool) and
you will discover a treasure box with a traveler's bow, an
effective early game weapon.

How to Obtain the Paraglider

Just after clearing up the last dungeon, come back to the Temple-of-Time to get the paraglider, that enables you to depart the "Great Plateau". Additionally, if you are something like us, you will be thinking just how in Hyrule to find the way to the top of the Temple-of-Time. The solution is in the image. (prior to you departing the tower, open up the chest to find the "soldier's bow".)

How to Get Concealed & Hidden Items

Before getting into the details about the "Great Plateau", it is worth understanding how to discover treasures in "Breath of the Wild". There're some basic guidelines that you need to stick to and you will begin making lucrative routines on the "Great Plateau".

CONSISTENTLY EXPLORE

If it appears obvious or puzzling, "Breath of the Wild" tasks you with determining just where to travel. It will certainly not show you.

Determining where to go is about checking out. Browse around. Take the scenic path. You are guaranteed to discover an item on your way less visited. Plus on the path often traveled. Yet again we think of it, in the room amongst the roads. Plus underwater. As well top of hills. As well as the air. Therefore, explore.

PROCEED WHERE YOU AREN'T SUPPOSE TO TRAVEL
Lots of hrs into "Breath of the Wild", we are yet amazed at how extensive the world is. take a line from any place around the map, and in just a moment you will find a thing to complete. Exploring constantly pays off and you are certain to come across secrets.

Around the "Great Plateau", there're several places you must check out before leaving. However in case you were to check out a map, you would observe that there is a great amount of land which you never in fact need to explore.

The place is packed with goodies. It is the best case of how wandering efforts will not go in vain. Make it a habit, find out where you are not really likely to go, then go there. You are guaranteed to stumble upon interesting items.

MAKE USE OF YOUR EYES AS WELL AS ABILITIES TO DISCOVER CONCEALED ITEMS

You have taken our suggestions, and you are now in the center of some huge, unexplored region. But you may be

wondering what the heck are you intended to now? Handful of things, really.

-Stroll around. Insane, right? However seriously, usually the simplest way to discover stuff is to just surf. "Breath of the Wild" has a large, wonderful world. Take time to amble through it and gather its concealed rewards. You will neglect an amazing trip if you are just driving between missions.

-Battle. In case you see a gang of opponents grouped around. Wipe them out. Every one of them. At least, you will find items drops and also monster parts that can be used to make elixirs (that we talk about in our "Breath of the Wild" cooking manual). Even better, in certain places, the baddies will likely be guarding the treasure. Eliminate the monstrosities, and you are prone to find a prize they were protecting.

-Utilize your abilities. Magnesis, stasis, as well as cryonis, the strengths you receive from a rune is modal. Push the L key, as well as the lens by which you see "Breath of the Wild" changes to teach you that you are executing something exceptional. When you are searching for secrets, these're useful resources since they can uncover concealed items. Just imagine, a treasure-chest seated in the bottom of a lake, much deeper than you can notice using your naked eye. Use magnesis, though, and you will view the outline of a thing you would never have realized was there.

Forest of Sprits & Hopper Pond

Forest of The Spirits covers the "Great Plateau's" upper 3rd region, covering The Hopper Pond as well as the Oman-Au-shrine. As we already mentioned above, you do not need to go through a majority of this region to finish your missions. However, you should, since the incentives are worth it.

VALUABLES IN A POND

Just outside the Forest-of-Spirits' north-east border, you will see the Oman-Au-shrine, where you acquire magnesis. And outside the shrine, there is a pond for you to discover treasure.

Utilize magnesis to raise the treasure-chest from the pond and get amber, that you can sell off or employ to make items afterwards in "Breath of the Wild".

ELIMINATING BOKOBLINS TO GET TREASURE

To the west of Oman-Au-shrine, you will discover a bokoblin camp. Eliminate all the opponents to open access to a

treasure-chest, in which you will find the "traveler's sword", a fantastic early game tool.

MUDDY POND

Just close to the corner from the Oman-Au-shrine, you will see a muddy pond. There're 2 things to gather here, utilizing the abilities you got from the "Great Plateau's spirit shrines".

Korok in mud

On a side of the pond, you will find a boulder linked through a chain with a tree stump. Employ magnesis to get the boulder and put it in the stump. A korok will show up and present you with a Korok seed, that can be used afterwards to increase your inventory.

TREASURE-CHESTS INSIDE THE MUD

On another side of mud pond opposite to the boulder, you will get a platform with 2 treasure-chests. Return towards the pond just outside of the Oman-Au-shrine. Employ magnesis to pick up and carry the lengthy, rectangle-shaped plank on to the ledge leading and up to the platform. Put it there, walk over the top of it, and open both of treasure-chests to collect 5 fire-arrows and 5 ice-arrows.

WITHIN THE FOREST-OF-SPIRITS

Our suggestions for the Forest-of -Spirits is easy: Explore each and every inch of it. You will find loads of things here from mushrooms to honey for stealth and creatures such as fish and frogs to gather. Try them all to cook.

Do not be worried about stuffing your inventory. It is unlike weapons and shield, where you have got a lower limit to the amount of things you can hold. You can have just as much as you would like.

KOROK FLOWER

Within the Forest-of-Spirits, you will find a huge hollow tree stump resting in the grass. In the centre, you will find a flower. Walk over it, and I will vanish. Find where it reappeared and do it again till a korok shows up to offer you a korok seed.

FLINT IN THE CAVE

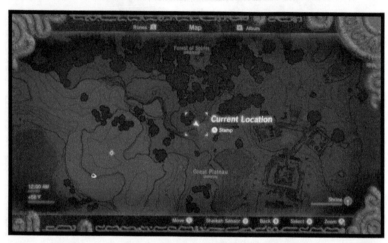

In a non-descript part of the forest, you will come across a small cave. Enter get some flint. Hit it using a weapon close to wood, and you will make your own campfire. It is

specifically beneficial in the cold region encircling Mount Hylia.

THE TEMPLE-OF-TIME AND NEIGHBOURHOOD

The Temple-of-Time looms over the "Great Plateau", and you will come across treasure within and all around it.

DESTRUCTIBLE WALL NEAR THE POND

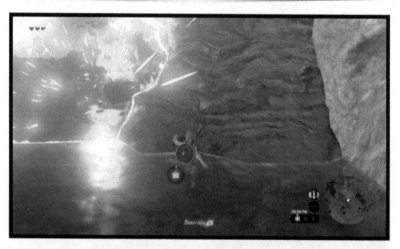

At the edge of the pond the place where a sword rests on an outcropping, part the wall structure will seem such as a assortment of loose stones. Go there and set off a bomb, and

the wall is going to disappear. Inside, you will get a treasure-chest having an opal.

HYLIAN-TROUSERS IN A TREASURE-CHEST

Inside among the structures outside the Temple-of-Time proper, you will get a treasure-chest having Hylian-trousers, a good update from the cruddy trousers you are wearing.

THE "TRAVELER'S BOW"

In the Temple-of-Time, you will get a treasure-chest having the traveler's-bow, an excellent update from low the level bows you will get from beating foes.

THE JAI-BAIJ-SHRINE AND NEIGHBOURHOOD

Inside the ruins surrounding the Jai-Baij-shrine, apply
magnesis to pick up a treasure-chest from a pond, and open
it up to find amber.

MOUNT-HYLIA AS WELL AS THE VICINITY

Mount-Hylia, the south-western area of the "Great Plateau", calls for defense against cold. The path to 2 shrines leads thru here, and there're secrets inside and just beyond its borders.

THE "BOKOBLIN TREE FORT" AND CHESTS

In the eastern side of Mount-Hylia, there is a tree fort stuffed with bokoblins. You are able to kill all of them from afar when you have sufficient arrows. You might as well simply utilize fire arrows (or fire up your normal arrows on the fire burning up on the ground) and aim for ropes that hold the ramp which leads up there.

Shoot your arrows as well as pillage the treasure-chests for amber and 5 arrows. There is also a big pillar, you are able to climb up near here having a treasure-chest at the top.

THE "WATERFALL TREASURE"

Get into Moun-Hylia's cold region from the west part of the map, take a left and stick to the way around the lake. Be ready to battle some chuchus.

Once you get to the cracked bridge, apply magnesis to pick up the steel platform and put it to cover the space in the bridge. now cross the bridge, take a left and maintain the

lake on your right. At the back side of the waterfall, you will come across soldier's broadsword, 5 arrows, 5 fire-arrows as well as a spiked-boko-bow.

Cooking

"Breath of the Wild" does not reveal its cooking method, that is weird, provided how essential it is. You can stroll upon the Old Man during your 1st hour, and he might let you know a thing ot two about cooking. Or perhaps you can skip this discussion all together and also play for many hrs before understanding it all by yourself. Do not do the second option. Begin cooking once you can.

EXACTLY WHAT WILL I COOK?

There're 2 broad types of items to cook in the game: elixirs and food. Regardless of what you are making, it functions the same exact way.

JUST HOW WILL I COOK?

Get to a metal bowl. Light fire beneath it if necessary. Push + to get to your inventory screen, and select up to 5 components to hold. Again approach the bowl, when prompted, push A to prepare food. It is that easy.

FOOD PREPARATION

Apples are definitely the most basic example of a prepared food's advantage. Consuming a raw apple replinish a tiny amount of your health almost equal to half of a heart. Preparing an apple becomes a baked apple, that restores an

entire heart. Cooking a couple of apples jointly produces simmered fruit, that restores 2 hearts however just occupies a single inventory slot. Exactly the same is true for the Hyrule-herb. Consume it raw, and it will recover 1 heart. Prepare it, and it will become fried wild-greens, that restores 2 hearts.

It is the basic benefit: Food preparation can make items better, stronger and effective.

This gets more complex, and that is where testing comes in. A lot of what you grab may add spice to your meals. Raw meats can get you hearts quickly. However uncooked meat put together with herbs can renew your stamina, as well. Or even give a protection or stealth raise.

COOKING ELIXIRS

Elixirs function just like food, only that they are liquid, and also they have got status effects. You will need 2 things to create an elixir: a critter along with a monster piece. Monster parts tend to be everywhere. Each time you eliminate a monster, it leaves a horn or perhaps a tooth or even some other grotesque body piece. Combine these using a critter; "Breath of the Wild's" expression for small animals similar to frogs, fireflies as well as lizards and you will develop an elixir.

COOKING TIPS

Cooking is all about testing. Do not hesitate to toss a bundle of things in a bowl and find out what happens. It may be a disaster, however you will be able to get more meat as well as apples.

More common tricks for cooking in "The Legend of Zelda: Breath of the Wild":

No matter what you're cooking, make sure to read the item descriptions when you're preparing your concoction. That is how you will realize, what you toss in the bowl is going to improve stealth or boost stamina or even defense.
Food and monster products do not mix.

Do not combine status effects. Anything you make will simply have one status impact, and you will end up throwing away the others if you combine them in.

If you prepare anything that you like, get around the product in the menu and also click on it to view the variety of ingredients. The Switch's one-button screen-shot function could not be simpler. Pick up one as well as refer back to it if you wish to create it once more.

You can easily cook your way to avoid tough battles. You possibly will not require better armor or even more hearts. You might only require a heart-meal which increases your defense.

Cook using ferries. They offer an amazing boost to your food.

Conclusion

Once you start to implement the strategies outlined there will be a much greater chance of success for you. In addition, you will find yourself beating parts of the game that you were once stuck on. This will not only make the game much more interesting and enjoyable but you will also realize a greater level of accomplishment. Good luck!

Free Bonus for our Readers

Thank-you for purchasing our eBook. We hope that in these readings you will have found value and helpful information. As an added bonus to your purchase please follow the "CLICK HERE" link below to sign-up for our free eBooks and guides program. Here you will receive free guides and resources for today's most popular games, mobile apps, and devices!

This is an exclusive and private offer for our customers. There is no purchase required, its 100% secure, and we will not send spam email of any kind. Just relevant strategies for today's most popular titles! To get started you can sing-up for free below.

CLICK HERE TO CLAIM YOUR FREE BONUS

CPSIA information can be obtained
at www.ICGtesting.com
Printed in the USA
LVHW05s0530140418
573475LV00013BB/807/P